"One of the best treatments of Java security issues I have ever had the pleasure to read. The advice offered in this book is sound and reasonable."

—Thomas A. Longstaff
Manager of Research & Development
CERT Coordination Center

"This book is mandatory reading for every user and developer of Webware. Its eye-opening analysis of the security risks provides timely realism amidst an otherwise mad dash to universal Net browsing."

—Peter G. Neumann
Principal Scientist, Computer Science Lab,
SRI International
Moderator of the Risks Forum
Author of *Computer-Related Risks*

"A provocative and useful discussion of security issues around Java and the Internet to date."

—Li Gong
Java Security Architect
JavaSoft

"... a tour de force.... clear and comprehensive discussions of the Java security model and various problems with its numerous implementations. It will make for enjoyable, and profitable, reading by all system administrators, Webmasters, and programmers—particularly in the corporate world.

If you surf, or if you maintain a Website, this book is for you. Buy it!"

—Gregory J. E. Rawlins
Associate Professor, Indiana University
Author of *Moths to the Flame:
The Seductions of Computer Technology*

"McGraw and Felten do a great job of presenting a thorough and understandable treatment of the complex security issues surrounding Java and other Web-related languages....This book is a must for anyone who uses Web browsers and related software, written by the experts who have practically defined the field of Java security."

—Michael Shoffner
Java developer
Prominence Dot Com

Java Security

Gary McGraw
&
Edward Felten

Wiley Computer Publishing

John Wiley & Sons, Inc.
New York • Chichester • Weinheim • Brisbane • Toronto • Singapore

Executive Publisher: Katherine Schowalter
Editor: Marjorie Spencer
Editorial Assistant: Margaret Hendrey
Managing Editor: Frank Grazioli
Text Design & Composition: Benchmark Productions, Inc.

This text is printed on acid-free paper.

Dr. McGraw's work is partially supported by DARPA Contract number F30602-95-C-0282. The views and conclusions contained in this book are those of the authors and should not be interpreted as representing the official policies, either expressed or implied, of the Defense Advanced Research Projects Agency or the U.S. government.

Research by Princeton's Safe Internet Programming Team is supported by donations from Bellcore, Sun Microsystems, and Microsoft.

Library of Congress Cataloging-in-Publication Data

McGraw, Gary, 1966-
     Java security : hostile applets, holes & antidotes / Gary McGraw
  and Edward Felten
        p.   cm.
     "Wiley Computer Publishing."
     Includes bibliographical references (p.).
     ISBN 0-471-17842-X (pbk. : alk. paper)
     1. Java (Computer program language) 2. Computer security.
  I. Felten, Edward. 1963-   .   II. Title.
  QA76.73.J38M354 1996
  005.8--dc20

                                   96-46121
                                     CIP

Printed in the United States of America
10 9 8 7 6 5 4 3 2

For our parents

Contents

Preface

The computer security issues surrounding Sun Microsystems, Inc.'s Java language are of great enough concern to us that we decided to write a book. Although this book gets somewhat technical in places, we have attempted to make the issues clear enough so that current Java users (including people whose only brush with Java is running the occasional applet while surfing the Web) can make sense of the often obscure and mysterious security concerns that Java raises. We do not intend to answer the question, Should you use Java? Nor do we intend to scare anyone away from Java. Instead, our goal is to inform you about very real risks so that you can form an intelligent Java use policy.

It is important to emphasize that to be a Java user you do not have to be a Java *programmer*. In fact, many people are Java users without realizing it. Whenever you use a Java-enabled browser like Netscape Navigator or Microsoft Internet Explorer to surf the Web, you become a Java user. We estimate that about 90 percent of Web users are, in this way, Java users. If you are a Java user, you need to know the risks.

The field of computers moves very quickly. One tricky aspect of writing a topical book relating to the Web is figuring out when to *stop* the action. This process can be likened to freeze-framing a picture of a movie. In that sense, this book is a snapshot of Java security. We hope we have succeeded in making it a useful way to learn about Java security. In addition to material about the current model and its problems, we have included much material about probable future developments.

Chapter 1 provides a quick and cursory introduction to Java. Pointers are provided to more thorough Java texts that cover the ins and outs of the entire Java language in more detail. This is, after all, not a book on Java per se, but is instead a book on Java security. The purpose of this

Chapter is to provide some context for the later discussion of Java's critical security implications and to introduce the central idea of the book: *weighing the benefits of Java use against the risks.*

Chapter 2 examines introduces the existing Java security model in some detail. As a prelude to our discussion, we introduce common security terminology (such as *denial of service attack*) so that you can better understand some of the jargon associated with computer security, what that jargon actually means in the real world, and how particular attacks can be delivered through Java applets. The three prongs of Java security defense are explained. These include the Byte Code Verifier, the Applet Class Loader, and the Java Security Manager. We also introduce the idea that Java security fundamentally relies on ensuring type safety. Java seems to have at least a rudimentary security policy, and it is apparent that the designers of Java gave security some thought. Chapter 2 answers the questions: What is Java's existing security policy? and, How well is it implemented in the current version of Java?

Chapter 3 delves more deeply into the existing Java security model by focusing attention on some of the well-publicized problems that have been discovered. This is where our discussion of hostile applets begins. We introduce some terminology that divides *hostile applets* into two camps—very dangerous *attack applets* that involve security breaches, and merely annoying malicious applets that are more of a nuisance than anything else. The purpose of Chapter 3 is to discuss attack applets and to elucidate just how secure Java really is *at the moment.* Java users must be educated about current problems in Java security if they are to make informed decisions regarding Java use. Some problems in the first release (post alpha and beta) of the Java Development Kit have been addressed through patching; others have not. We will discuss both sets of problems in some detail.

Fundamentally less dangerous but still annoying, malicious applets are the topic of Chapter 4. We provide some general examples of malicious applets and describe what exactly they do. Unfortunately there are many unscrupulous individuals on the Net who are more than happy to include Java in their list of offensive weapons. Our mission is to make Java users aware of common classes of attacks.

Chapter 5 has two overall goals, both of which are meant to impact the Java security situation positively. The first is to suggest some high-level antidotes for Java security concerns that are not tied to particular attacks. Experts in computer security have pointed out several global deficiencies in the Java approach to security. Fixing some of these things would certainly improve the model. High-level concerns addressed in part one of Chapter 5 include: programming language issues, formal analysis of Java, applet logging, and decompilation. Hopefully some of the high-level concerns we raise in Chapter 5 will be fixed in the near future. In the meantime, we can offer some guidelines for safer Java use that can be applied *now*. These guidelines make up the second part of Chapter 5. If you only have time to read one section of this book, "Guidelines for Java Users" (page 133) should be the one.

We conclude with some hints about what may happen to the Java security model in the future. The JavaSoft division of Sun Microsystems is working hard to improve the existing security situation (which currently has, as we discuss throughout this book, some rather serious flaws). The browser companies, Netscape and Microsoft, are also working to improve Java security since many of Java's security policies get defined by the browser. Cool things that should improve Java security will likely include digitally signed applets, an in-depth analysis of the Java security model, and better Class Loaders and Security Managers.

We hope that this book is both informative and useful. Making intelligent decisions regarding the use of Java (especially in business and other mission-critical systems) requires some knowledge of the current risks. Our goal is to disclose those risks—and countermeasures to curtail them—as clearly and objectively as possible. Armed with the knowledge that we present in this book, Java users and site managers can make better Java use policies.

Acknowledgments

This book is a collaborative effort in more ways than one. Not only did the authors work together closely, but we also sought input from many other people. We are grateful for the help we received.

Reliable Software Technologies (http://www.rstcorp.com) is a great place to work. The intellectually stimulating environment makes going to work interesting and fun. Many people at RST read drafts of the book or helped in other ways. They include: Jon Beskin (resident philosopher and graph generator), Anup Ghosh (fellow security researcher), Kara Joy, Lora Kassab (who not only read several chapters, but also wrote some of the Java code in the book), Rich Mills, Jeff Payne (RST's forward-thinking CEO), Adam Paul, Mike Pease (PC screen dump guy), Melissa Rau, Cathy Streightiff, and Jeff Voas (who brought together RST's excellent research group).

The members of Princeton University's Safe Internet Programming Team (http://www.cs.princeton.edu/sip) also provided valuable input. Besides wading through several drafts, the Princeton team was responsible for raising many of the key issues in Java security. Special thanks to Drew Dean and Dan Wallach (co-founders of the Princeton team) and Dirk Balfanz (the team's Internet Explorer expert). Princeton's Computer Science department provides a wonderful environment for discovering and exploring new research topics.

We would also like to thank: Lee Badger, Jeff Cook, and Peter Churchyard, all of Trusted Information Systems; Tom Cargill, independent consultant and discoverer of two security flaws; David Hopwood, discoverer of several attack applets; Ivan Krusl, a graduate student at Purdue's COAST lab; Mark La Due, graduate student at Georgia Tech and maintainer of the Hostile Applet Home Page; Tom Longstaff, research director at the CERT Coordination Center; Marianne Mueller, Java developer, security expert, and long-suffering target of press inquiries at JavaSoft; Jim Roskin, Netscape's Java security expert; and Mike Shoffner, Java developer at Prominence Dot Com. Li Gong, security architect at Javasoft, provided especially valuable input and kept us pointed in the right direction at times.

Wiley's staff did an excellent job shepherding this book through the editing and production process. Special thanks to Marjorie Spencer and Frank Grazioli who went out of their way to make this project go smoothly. Also thanks to the rest of the team at Wiley.

Finally, and most importantly, we're grateful to our families for putting up with us while we worked on the book. Amy Barley and babyman Jack suffered through thesis-mode take #2. Laura Felten and Claire coped admirably with Ed's new-found book-writing habit. Without the support of our families, this book would not have been possible.

Chapter 1

Do You Know Where Your Browser Is Pointing?

Why Java security is important

There are an estimated forty million users of Netscape Navigator (Netscape) and Microsoft Internet Explorer.* A majority of the users of these browsers are also Java users, whether they know it or not. Since Java is built in to Netscape and Internet Explorer, if you use either of these products, *you* are a Java user.

All Java users are taking security risks. Because of the way Java works, computer security issues are a fundamental concern. Most Java code is automatically downloaded across the network and runs *on your machine*. This makes it very important to limit the sorts of things that this kind of Java program can do. A hostile Java program could trash your machine. Because Java is inherently Web-based, it provides crackers an easy way to implement a Trojan Horse—a program that may seem innocent enough on the surface, but is actually filled with well-armed

---

* To be fair, significantly more World Wide Web users use the Netscape product than use the Microsoft product today.

1

Greeks. Fortunately, the creators of Java have made a good effort to protect users from these hazards. They have not always been successful.

This book is meant to educate Java users about the risks that they incur by surfing the World Wide Web with Java-enabled browsers. This chapter provides a gentle introduction to Java, and explains why Java is potentially dangerous. Although the next few sections touch on some aspects of Java security, people who already know about Java may want to skip ahead to page 24.

Executable Content

The Java programming environment from Sun Microsystems is designed for developing programs that run on many different kinds of networked computers. Because of its multi-platform capabilities, Java shows great promise for relieving many of the headaches that developers encounter when they are forced to migrate code between different types of operating systems. Code that is written in Java should run on *all* of the most popular platforms—everything ranging from Macintosh and Windows/Intel machines to Linux and Solaris boxes.

A nice side-effect of Java's built-in portability is that one special kind of Java program (popularly known as an *applet*) can be attached to a Web page. More technically speaking, applets are embedded into a Web page's *hypertext markup language* (HTML) definition and "interpreted" by Java-savvy browsers.* Such Java-enabled browsers automatically download and begin running any Java applet they find embedded in a Web page. Java code's ability to run on many diverse platforms makes such "magic" possible.

---

* Both the popular Netscape Navigator 2.0x browser (as well as the recently released Navigator 3) and the Microsoft Internet Explorer 3.0 browser are capable of running Java applets. Other browsers promise Java capability soon.

The ability to dynamically download and run Java code over the Net has led some computer pundits to proclaim that the age of truly component-based software development may actually have arrived. The idea is that instead of buying huge monolithic word processing behemoths with hundreds of obscure features that most users will never need, users can instead "create" a personal word processor on-the-fly out of Java building blocks. This modern sort of programming is akin to building a large toy ship out of Lego blocks. Or, more realistically, the process of creating a component-based software product could be likened to building a highway bridge out of standardized structural components.

Thinking even farther into the future, one can imagine a fundamentally new kind of computer document that contains the word processing, spreadsheet, and database software that were used to create it. Using a document's embedded components, a writer or editor could modify the document on any platform. The built-in components would allow different people using different machines to edit the document without worrying about the kind of computer they were using or file type compatibility issues. If Java is developed to its full potential, this future world may not be far off.

The new idea behind all of these exciting aspects of Java is simple—sending around data that can be automatically executed wherever it arrives, anywhere on the Net. Java is an implementation of *executable content* [Bank, 1995]. This powerful idea opens up many new possibilities on the World Wide Web. For the first time it is possible to have users download from the Web and locally run a program written in a truly common programming language. Full-fledged Web-based programs written in Java are just around the corner.*

---

* Java has some competition as an environment for creating executable content. Other languages with a similar bent are: JavaScript, Safe-Tcl, Telescript, Word macros, Excel macros, ActiveX, and Postscript. Many of the security lessons in this book apply to those languages as well.

These features of Java are certainly exciting. However, Java's fantastic potential is mitigated by serious security concerns. Security is always an issue when computers are networked. Realistically speaking, there is no such thing as a computer system that is 100% secure [Cheswick and Bellovin, 1994]. Users of networked computers must weigh the benefits of being connected to the world against the risks that they incur simply by connecting.

One of the key selling points of Java is its use as a "cross-platform" language for creating executable content in the highly-interconnected world of the Internet. Simply by using a Web browser, a Web surfer can take advantage of Java's amazing cross-platform capability. Of course, the activity of locally running code created and compiled somewhere else has important security implications. These implications are the focus of this book.

The same risks and benefits that apply to connecting to the Internet itself directly apply to using the Java language. As you will see, these concerns become particularly critical when "surfing the Web." The same technology that allows Java applets to enliven once-static Web pages also allows unscrupulous applet designers to invade an unsuspecting Java user's machine. With Java applets showing up everywhere, and 40 million people using Java-enabled browsers, it pays to know where you are pointing your browser.

The Network as Computer

Networking has changed the face of computing. In order for a computer to perform up to its potential in the '90s, it almost certainly must be connected to the global network. In fact, some computer visionaries, most notably Scott McNealy of Sun Microsystems, claim that the entire future of computing lies in the network and not in the machines themselves. McNealy's has been attributed with the famous line: "the network *is* the computer." The move towards a realization of the network as computer has been significantly furthered by Java.

The Internet: A World of Connections

Since its birth in the early '70s as a twelve-node network called the ARPANET,* the Internet has exponentially exploded into a world-wide network that provides a central piece of the planet's information infrastructure. Figure 1.1 shows the growth pattern of the Internet from its humble 12-host beginnings through today's some five million registered addresses.

Connecting computers together in a network allows computer users to share data, programs, and each others' computational resources. Once a computer is put on a network, it is possible to "log in" to a remote machine in order to retrieve data, or to use its CPU cycles and other resources. Along with this ability comes concern about security. Computer security specialists worry about issues such as:

- who is allowed to connect to a particular machine
- how to determine whether or not access credentials are being faked
- how to limit the access a remote machine or user has to the host machine.

Whenever machines are networked, these concerns must be addressed.

The Internet, being the world's largest network of machines, has encouraged research into these security issues. Mechanisms now in place go beyond simple password authentication, to *firewalls*, and security checking tools such as SATAN [Farmer, 1996]. Because there are so many machines connecting to the Net, computer security is becoming more and more important. New ideas in computer security are constantly becoming available on the Net. Security approaches currently in

---

* ARPA (now DARPA) is an acronym for the United States Department of Defense's Advanced Research Project Agency who sponsored initial research on networking computers. DARPA currently supports many research projects in computer security, including work by the authors.

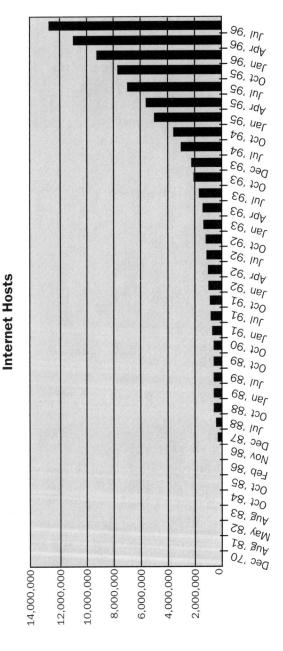

Figure 1.1 Growth of the Internet since its early days as the ARPANET. Data from the Internet Society (**http://www.isoc.org**).

preliminary use include encryption-based authentication, encrypted communications, and intrusion detection based on Artificial Intelligence (AI) [Hughes, 1995; Garfinkle and Spafford, 1996].

The Web: Making the Internet Enticing

One of the driving forces behind the exponential growth of the Internet in the last five years has been the introduction of the World Wide Web. In 1992, Tim Berners-Lee, a British researcher at the CERN physics facility in Europe, invented a new way to use the Internet. His invention introduced hypertext markup language (HTML) and Web browsing to the world. In 1993, Marc Andreesen helped to write the Mosaic Web browser while affiliated with the National Center for Supercomputer Applications (NCSA). He later co-founded the company now known as Netscape Communications. Though it may be hard to believe, the Web is only a few years old.

Before the invention of the Web, the Internet was almost exclusively text-based. Researchers used it to transfer files to one another, and to keep in touch via e-mail. After the Web was invented, it suddenly became possible to see graphical pages sent across the Net by Web servers. These Web pages can include pictures, sound, video, and text as well as *hyper-links* to related pages. A Web browser provides an easy-to-use, intuitive interface for "surfing," or traveling around the Web, visiting other people's pages. Figure 1.2 shows how a typical Web page looks when viewed with the Netscape browser. Note that the page includes a Java applet.

Ease of use is partially responsible for the astonishing numbers of Web users, and perhaps the sense of safety that most Web users seem to enjoy. In addition, creating Web pages is a relatively simple process. HTML editors like Netscape Navigator Gold, and Microsoft Frontpage make the job especially easy. Given one of these editors and a Web server, you have all the pieces you need to create your own Web site. An alternative to using an HTML editor is to write HTML code directly. Either way, this

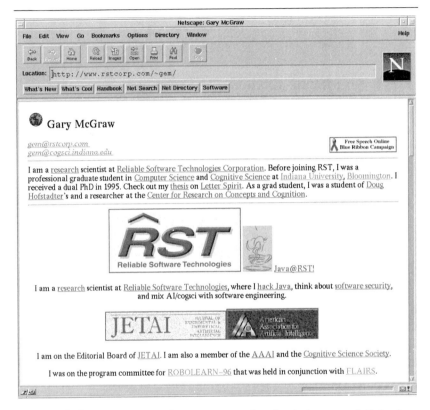

Figure 1.2 Netscape is the most popular "web browser." It is Java ready by default. Other browsers include Microsoft's Internet Explorer (also Java-enabled) and Spyglass's Mosaic. This is the top half of the author's home page. Note that there is a Java applet embedded in this page. Animated steam rises from the Java cup situated to the right of the RST logo.

snazzy new HTML facade makes the Internet more attractive than ever before.

As can be seen in Figure 1.3, the Web has grown just as quickly as the Internet itself. The figure charts a conservative estimate of the number

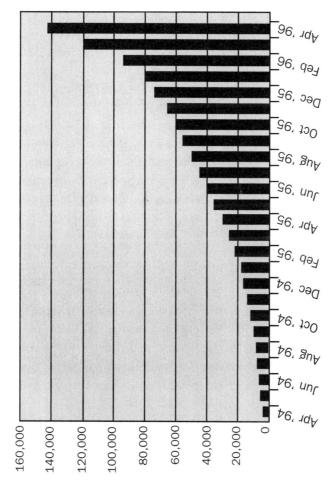

Figure 1.3 Growth of the World Wide Web since its introduction in 1993, captured from URL http://webcrawler.com/WebCrawler/Facts/Size.html.

of Web servers on the Net. It is these servers that allow people to make Web pages available to everyone. The figure does not properly reflect the number of Web pages that are out there, which some people number in the tens of millions. Keep in mind that a server has the potential to serve hundreds or even thousands of pages for multiple users simultaneously.

Java: Spicing Up the Web

HTML-based Web pages are certainly a big step up from using the obscure text-based UNIX incantations of **ftp**, **news**, **gopher**, **wais**, and **telnet** to get around on the Net. But they also have a major drawback. Much like the page that you are reading now, Web pages are static. Wouldn't it be better to have interactive Web pages that dynamically change themselves according to feedback from a user? Wouldn't it be better to program your Web pages to accept input, compute results, and then display them?

This sort of dynamic activity should ring a bell. After all, programming languages allow people to program machines to do just these sorts of things. Why not make a programming language for the Web?

That is the essence of Java. Java is a full-featured programming language that allows programmers to compose executable content for the Web. The Java language is designed to be usable on all platforms. Cross-platform compatibility has always been a stumbling block in previous attempts to create programming languages for executable content. Executable content is only useful if it can be executed on all platforms without porting and recompiling!

In order to allow Java to run on a computer, the administrator must first install a Java *Virtual Machine* (VM). The Java VM interprets Java instructions and translates them into machine-specific instructions. This allows Java to be run on many different kinds of machine.* Using an

---

* Netscape Navigator 2.0x Netscape Navigator 3.0, and Microsoft Internet Explorer 3.0 each include a complete Java VM that can interpret the Java byte code making up a Java applet.

interpreter allows Java to get around problems that have plagued the C programming language, making it less platform-independent than its designers intended. Unlike C programs, Java programs are not hampered by machine-dependent structures such as:

- *byte ordering* (low or high endian)
- *pointer size* (16 or 32 bit)
- *integer size* (8 bit, 16 bit, or 32 bit)

As an interpreted language, Java is shielded from these platform-specific elements of programming. Each Java VM is written to a specific platform, and translates the more generic Java instructions into platform-specific instructions.

Java has upped the ante on the Web. The best Web pages now include Java applets that do everything from displaying selectable news tickers to providing front-end *graphical user interfaces* (GUI's) for internal databases. There are even some Web-based video games written in Java. Java applets are quickly becoming commonplace.

The Promise of Java

Java is by far the most popular implementation of Web-based executable content concept. Lesser-known competitors include JavaScript, Safe-Tcl, Telescript, Word macros, Excel macros, ActiveX, and Postscript. Any document-embedded scripting language that can be transferred around the Net and run on different machines falls under the classification of executable content.* Propelled by the marketing powers of Sun Microsystems and Netscape, the Java wave is still building. Java avoids the interactive content limitations that were built in to forms and CGI

---

* Note that many of the lessons of this book apply directly to all of these executable content languages since the crux of the security problem is the idea of running untrusted code safely.

scripts.* Java's power lies in the ability to program complete applications in a real programming language that can then be dynamically distributed and run by virtually any user over the Web.

Java in a Demitasse

The security concerns raised in this book apply equally to both Java users and Java developers. Using Java is as easy as surfing the Web. The simple use of Netscape, Internet Explorer, or any other Java-enabled browser to run Java applets is a risky activity. In order to really understand these risks, it is important to gain a deeper understanding of how Java really works. Here is a short but thorough introduction to the Java language.

The Java development environment comprises three major components:

1. a programming language that compiles into an intermediate, architecturally-neutral format called *byte code*
2. the Java Virtual Machine that interprets the byte code
3. an execution environment that runs on the interpreter and provides some base classes useful for building complete applications

Figure 1.4 shows how these three parts of the Java environment work together to provide executable content for the Web. The Java Developers Kit (JDK) is provided free to all. It includes the three parts of the Java environment outlined here. To get your own copy, point your browser to URL **http://java.sun.com**.

Because Java byte code runs on the Java Virtual Machine, it is possible to run Java code on any platform to which the VM has been ported.

---

* These limitations had mainly to do with the fact that CGI scripts run on the server side, whereas Java applets run on the client side.

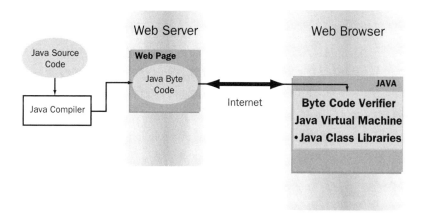

Figure 1.4 How the Java environment works over the web. Java source code files are compiled into Java byte code using the Java compiler (javac). The Java byte code (in applet form) can be embedded into a web page. Web surfers can use the applet by surfing to a web page with their browser. The browser processes Java byte code by first verifying it, then dynamically linking in any needed Java classes. The Java Virtual Machine allows the machine-independent byte code to be run on a large number of different platforms.

Some Web browsers, such as Netscape and Internet Explorer include an encapsulated version of the Java VM. Using their built-in VMs, such Java-ready browsers can automatically download and execute Java applets when a user accesses an HTML Web page with the **<APPLET>** tag.

The Java Language

One of the first public introductions to Java came in the form of a white paper released by Sun (and since updated many times) [Sun Microsystems, 1995]. An especially pithy sentence from that document attempts to describe the fundamental aspects of Java all at once. It reads:

> *Java*: *A simple, object-oriented, distributed, interpreted, robust, secure, architecture neutral, portable, high-performance, multi-threaded, and dynamic language.*

Quite a collection of buzzwords. This book is concerned mostly with the security claim, of course. But in order to understand the implications of Java for computer security, you need to grasp the other important characteristics of the language first.

As the quote claims, Java has many interesting features. They will be briefly introduced here. Pointers to more information on Java can be found on page 22. The Java language is:

> *Object-oriented*: *Unlike C++ which is an objectivized version of C, Java is intrinsically object-oriented. This changes the focus of programming from the old procedural way of thinking (e.g., C and Pascal) to a new data-centric model. In this new model, data objects possess associated methods. Methods perform actions on data objects. Every Java program is composed of one or more* classes. *Classes are collections of data objects and the methods that manipulate these data objects. Each class is one kind of object. Classes are arranged in a hierarchy such that a* subclass inherits *behavior and structure from its superclass. Object oriented languages were designed using the physical world as a metaphor. Classes communicate with each other in much the same way that real physical objects in the world interact.*

> *Strongly typed*: *This means that a Java program cannot arbitrarily access the host computer's memory. Memory access by Java programs is limited to specific, controlled areas having particular representations.*

Java's runtime environment includes name spaces. This allows local trusted classes to be separated from untrusted classes loaded off the network. Packages in Java are collections of classes. Type safety is verified at load time by the Byte Code Verifier (see Chapter 2). In addition, runtime checks on type safety (such as array bound overflow, type incompatibility, and local-versus-remote code security policy) are all handled by the Java VM.

Multi–threaded: *Java programs can execute more than one task at the same time. For example, a multimedia Java applet may want to play a sound file, display a picture, and download a file all at once. Since Java is multi-threaded, it supports the concurrent execution of many light-weight processes. An obvious benefit of this capability is that it improves the performance of multimedia applications at the user end. Java's built-in support for threads makes designing such applications far easier than it is in C and C++. Primitives for synchronization are also provided in Java.*

Java has other important characteristics adapted from modern programming languages such as Scheme (a superior dialect of Lisp). In particular, Java uses:

Garbage collection: *Memory management is usually handled in one of two ways. The old-fashioned approach is to have a program allocate and de-allocate memory itself. This approach allows all sorts of insidious errors and hard-to-squash bugs. C, for instance, uses this method. By contrast, Lisp introduced the concept of garbage collection. Garbage collection requires the language to keep track of memory usage, providing a way to reference objects. When items are no longer needed, the memory where they live is automatically dereferenced (freed) so it is available for other uses. Java provides a fast, efficient garbage collector that uses multi-threading to run silently in the background. Java's memory management approach has important implications for the security model since it prevents problems associated with dangling pointers.*

No pointers: *This is also a feature of Java's modern memory management scheme. Instead of allowing access to memory through pointers, memory is managed by reference. The crucial difference between references and pointers is that references cannot be manipulated through arithmetical means (as can pointers). This eliminates many potential bugs. Pointers are one of the most bug-prone aspects of C and C++. Eliminating pointers has the effect of making Java a much more reliable and safer language.*

Exception handling: *This defines how the program will manage an error condition. For example, if a Java program tries to open a file that it has no privilege to read, an exception will be thrown. Exception throwing and catching is a system for gracefully managing runtime errors which might otherwise crash a system.*

Dynamic linking: *Software modules (classes in Java) are linked together as they are needed. The Java language knows where it should look for classes that need to be linked while a Java program runs. By contrast, C has a linking phase during which all needed constructs are linked before the program is run. The linking phase in C is static since library functions are assembled together with other code into a complete executable at compile time. Dynamic linking makes it easier to keep Java programs up-to-date since the latest version of a class will always be used. Because the static linking phase is eliminated, Java programs do not require preprocessing, using, for example, #include statements. Java finds classes that it needs by searching for them in locations specified in the* CLASSPATH *environment variable.*

Java is a relatively simple language. This is especially apparent when Java is compared with C and C++ [Daconta, 1996]. In C, there are often many possible ways to do the same thing. Java tries to provide only one language mechanism to perform a particular task. Also, Java provides no macro support. Though some programmers like using macros, macros often end up making programs much harder to read and debug.

The designers of Java made their language simple by removing a number of features that can be found in C and C++. Things that were removed include: the **goto** statement, the use of header files, the **struct** and **union** constructs, operator overloading, and multiple inheritance. Together with the elimination of pointers, removal of these aspects of C and C++ make Java easier to use. This should result in more reliable code.*

Portable Byte Code and the Java Virtual Machine

The second major component of the Java development environment is the Java Virtual Machine. The VM makes Java's cross-platform capabilities possible. In order to run Java byte code on a new platform, all that is required is a working VM. Once the VM has been ported to a platform, all Java byte code is guaranteed to run properly.

Making a byte code/VM pair that works well on many varied platforms involves setting a few things in stone. Java has variables that are of fixed size and of fixed format. An **Integer** in Java is *always* 32 bits, no matter what the word size of the machine running Java. Making variables machine-independent and compiler-independent is crucial to making Java truly portable. The very different way in which variables are managed on different C platforms causes no end of portability problems for C programmers.

The VM also makes use of symbolic data stored inside of Java byte code files. Java byte code contains enough symbolic information to allow some analysis of the byte code before it is run. This is one way the Java environment ensures that Java's language rules have been followed by the compiler—something critical to security. Rules checked include, for example, type safety rules, ensuring that certain things claiming to be of a certain type actually are of that type. Since the Java byte code Verifier is a critical part of the security model, it is discussed in detail in Chapter 2.

---

* Some experts' opinions about Java and reliability differ, however. For an interesting critique of Java see [Lewis, 1996].

Using a virtual machine has obvious important repercussions for the Java approach. The VM makes portability possible, and it helps to ensure some of Java's security features. Since Java is an interpreted language, speed could be an issue. Interpreted languages are inherently slow because each command must be translated to native machine code before it can be run. With a compiler, this work is all done ahead of time, when an executable is created for some particular platform. Without the new just-in-time (JIT) compilers, Java's interpreted code is about 20 times slower than native C code.

Reusable Class Modules

The third part of the Java development environment is a set of pre-defined classes that implement basic functionality. The JDK includes, for example, an Abstract Window Toolkit (AWT). These classes provide a complete set of graphical user interface (GUI) tools for creating windows, dialogue boxes, scrollbars, buttons, etc. Java also includes classes for full network support that provide application program interfaces (APIs) for sockets, streams, URLs and datagrams. A POSIX-like I/O system with APIs for files, streams, and pipes makes the environment comfortable for experienced UNIX programmers. Classes are grouped together into packages according to their functionality. Table 1.1 lists the packages included in the Java Developers Kit (JDK) version 1.0.2.

Table 1.1 Packages supplied by the JDK provide multi-platform primitives from which complete applications can be assembled. *Java in a Nutshell* is an excellent reference describing these packages [Flanagan, 1996].

java.applet	The Applet class.
java.awt	Abstract Windowing Toolkit: The AWT provides graphics, GUI components, and layout managers.
java.awt.image	Image processing classes.
java.awt.peer	Interface definitions for GUI components and platforms.

Table 1.1 Continued

java.io	Input/Output classes: A relatively large number of classes for I/O.
java.lang	Central Java language classes: Defines **Object**, **Class**, and primitive types.
java.net	Networking classes.
java.util	Miscellaneous but critical classes: These classes are required for many others.

The pre-defined Java classes provide enough functionality to write full-fledged programs in Java. Using the pre-defined classes as primitives, it is possible to construct higher-level classes and packages. Many such home grown packages are already available on the Net.

Applets versus Applications

There is a strict and important difference between two types of Java programs—applets and applications. Java applets are usually, though not necessarily, small programs meant to be run in the context of a Web browser. Applets are executable content. Obviously, applets involve the most security concerns of any Java programs. In fact, Java's security policies exist in order to make applets feasible. The Java run-time enforces severe limitations on the things that applet classes may do [Sun Microsystems, 1996a]. See Chapter 2 for details.

Java applications have no such restrictions. Applications use the complete power of Java. Just like C programs, Java applications can read and write files and manipulate memory. Java presents an advantage as a development language even if you discard its applet capabilities. Since the Java language is defined in a platform-independent manner, the usual difficulties encountered when porting programs simply disappear. This makes Java appealing even if security problems make Web-based applets too risky.

A Simple Example—twice A simple example serves to illustrate the difference between applets and applications. This Java program can be written in both forms. Here it is as an application:

```
public class HelloWorld{
        public static void main(String[] args){
                System.out.println("Hello World!");
        }
}
```

Experienced programmers will recognize the purpose of this program immediately. Here is the same program written as an applet:

```
import java.awt.Graphics;
public class HelloWorld extends java.applet.Applet {
        public void init() {
                resize(150, 25);
        }
        public void paint(Graphics g) {
                g.drawstring("Hello World!", 50, 25);
        }
}
```

Notice the lack of **main()** in the applet. Also notice that the applet extends the Applet class, while the application defines an entirely new class for itself. In order to run, the applet needs to be embedded in an HTML document with the **<APPLET>** tag. This can be done as follows:

```
<HTML>
<HEAD>
```

```
<TITLE> A Simple Program </TITLE>
</HEAD>
<BODY>
Here is the output of my program:
<APPLET CODE="HelloWorld.class" WIDTH=150 HEIGHT=25>
</APPLET>
</BODY>
</HTML>
```

The applet also requires a Java-enabled browser to run. On the other hand, the application only requires the Java interpreter. Note that the JDK includes a standalone interpreter. That means a Web server and a Net connection are not required for using Java.

Although this example applet is entirely benign, and not very powerful, it is possible to write very powerful applets that do a large number of things. Since the book is fundamentally concerned with security, the focus will be on Java applets.

Java as Safe for Untrusted Code

Since a Java-enabled Web browser allows Java code to be downloaded and run on a local machine, security is of critical concern. Java applets are exceptionally easy to download—sometimes without even knowing it, and not always voluntarily. Because Java makes running external, untrusted code a normal event, using Java involves taking on a significant amount of risk.

Security risks fall into four basic categories: system modification, invasion of privacy, denial of service, and antagonism. These four categories of risk are discussed in detail in Chapter 2. The first two of our risk categories are handled moderately well by Java. The second two are not. Risks are particularly egregious in Java since exploiting vulnerabilities is simply a matter of booby-trapping a Web page with a malicious applet or two. Chapter 4 discusses malicious applets. Java applets with bad intentions are the equivalent of every security administrator's night-mare—exploitation scripts [Garfinkle and Spafford, 1996].

Java's designers are well aware of many of the risks associated with exe-cutable content. To combat these risks, Java was specifically designed with security concerns in mind. The main goal was to address the security issue head-on so that naive users (most of the 40 million users of Netscape) would not have to become security experts just to surf the Web.

Java presents a three-tiered approach to security. At a general level, the three tiers are:

- restricted access to file systems and the network
- restricted access to browser internals
- a set of load time and runtime checks to verify that byte code is following the rules.

The Java security model will be detailed in Chapter 2. Many claims have been made about the security of the Java language. We will try to separate reality from marketing hype in order to better understand the Java security model.

Where to Find More Information on Java

Java on the Web

An excellent place to start learning about Java is the Web itself. The first URL to check is JavaSoft **http://java.sun.com**. Also useful is Gamelan **http://www.gamelan.com**. MindQ sells a very good CD-ROM that provides a multimedia introduction to programming Java applets and applications. See their Web page for details **http://www.mindq.com**. MindQ is working with the authors on a Java Security CD-ROM as well. To discover some of the many other

Java resources on the Net, search for Java at Yahoo! **http://www .yahoo.com** or on AltaVista **http://www.altavista.digital.com**. Also see two collections of secu rity related Java links put together by the authors at **http://www.rstcorp.com/java-security.html** and at **http://www.cs .princeton.edu/sip**.

Java Books

If you crave a paper copy of something, or if you need a reference book to rifle through when you are learning about Java, you might prefer a Java book. The number of books on Java is growing almost as fast as the Web itself. For a large list see **http://lightyear.ncsa .uiuc.edu/~srp/java/javabooks.html**. We have had a chance to use a few of them as Java coders. Here are five, with a brief review for each.

> ***Core Java*** *[Cornell and Horstmann, 1996] This is a good book; big, but definitely useful. It is full of comparisons to C++ and Visual Basic, including useful pictures. There is not, however, a list of the standard eight Java packages, which is an inconvenience. To make up for this, the authors provide implementations for other classes that are not in the Java libraries, but are commonly used.*

> ***Java!*** *[Ritchey, 1995] This was the first reasonable book about Java to come out. It provides a good introduction to Java with a few limited examples. However, it has become out-dated and less useful than some of the other Java books listed here.*

> ***Java for C/C++ Programmers*** *[Daconta, 1996] This book is a good reference for people who understand C++ and are familiar with the pros and cons of the C++ and the object-oriented approach. The side-by-side comparison of C++ and Java is useful.*

> ***Java in a Nutshell*** *[Flanagan, 1996] This book seems to be everyone's favorite—probably because it is so useful. The book pro-*

vides an extensive API for the packages provided by Java. This makes it excellent for a quick desk-side reference. There are examples for almost everything discussed. It is useful both for beginners and more advanced Java programmers.

Java Unleashed *[Sams.net, 1996] This book is useful for Web development, and for interacting with Netscape and HotJava. It is not the best for a quick reference, since it is bulky. But for Internet-specific topics, this book could be the most useful. Prior knowledge of Java is required to get the most out of this book.*

Java Has Its Price

Java is most definitely cool. Having programs embedded in Web pages that can run on any platform is an excellent idea. But in order to get this power, users take a great deal of risk.

A Web surfer can click to a Web page with an embedded applet that immediately and automatically begins executing. Often, the user *doesn't even know this is happening*. This situation might not be so bad if the Java environment being used were 100% secure. But to make Java really secure would require making it completely impotent.*

There is a price that must be paid for the power of executable content. This price is very similar to the price that must be paid in order to connect to the Internet in the first place. The bill is payable in terms of risk and exposure to attack. The question is, how much risk are you willing to take? How critical is the information on your machine? Our goal in writing this book is to arm the reader with the data that is needed to make an informed, intelligent decision about

---

* Keep in mind that the most secure machine is a machine that is kept "off" at all times and is locked away in a room. Of course a machine this secure is also useless.

Java use.

Downloading Mystery Code

How often do you download executable code from various unknown sites on the Net? Do you think about where the code is coming from and who wrote it? Do you know what it will do before you run it?

Even if you are particularly cautious about downloading binaries from the Net, the answers to the questions raised will undoubtedly soon change. Applets are cropping up everywhere. At the moment, surfing the Web with a Java-enabled browser is tantamount to downloading and running arbitrary binaries, albeit with some level of security provided by Java. Deciding whether or not this is a good idea is an important decision that is as personal as a financial investment strategy.

It is worth repeating that there is no such thing as *perfect* security. This is true for any system on the Internet, not just systems using Java. Someone will always be probing Java security, trying to find new ways around or through the existing system. In the real world, all you can expect is *reasonable* security. The solution to this conundrum is finding an acceptable tradeoff between functionality and security.

Playing the Cost/Benefit Game

The Internet is a dangerous playground. Java offers an intriguing approach to the problem of security by neither ignoring it entirely (as most languages do) nor being completely paralyzed by it. Deciding what level of risk to incur is really a matter of weighing the potential costs of using Java against the clear benefits of using Java. Making an informed and intelligent decision requires understanding both aspects of the situation. Business people are always weighing costs and benefits when making complicated decisions. The same sort of careful consideration that goes into forming a business plan should also go into the formulation of a Java use policy.

The Java hype machine has been exceptionally good at broadcasting the benefits of Java. They have been successful largely because Java really does have vast potential. On the other hand, the advertising has been slightly less straightforward about the risks. This may be because the risks are complicated and sometimes hard to understand. Computer security is a new field to many users, and few people are aware of all the issues. As the Net grows, the Web is woven. As Java applets become ubiquitous, it behooves us to become more aware of security issues. Ignorance is not bliss.

Assessing the Risks

Now that the basics of the Java environment have been covered, you are ready to examine Java security in earnest. It is only after understanding what the security model is, how it works, and how it doesn't, that you can truly begin to assess the security situation.

People should think carefully about using Java even casually with a Java-enabled browser. This book will present some of the facts associated with Java security so that you may decide when, where, and how to use Java. Unfortunately, there is no black-and-white answer to the question: *Should I use Java?*

Chapter 2

The Java Security Model
Making applets safe

Java is designed so that programs can be dynamically loaded over the network and run locally. This very powerful new paradigm promises to change the face of computing as we know it. A browser that can interpret Java byte code (such as Netscape or Internet Explorer) can download and locally execute applets that are embedded in a Web page. This activity of downloading and executing is completely automatic, requires no user approval, and sometimes occurs without the user even knowing. Remember, by simply pointing your browser at a Web page containing an applet, you start Java. Any applet started in this fashion is not required to advertise its presence. More and more Java applets appear on the Web every day. Soon applets will be ubiquitous. This means that surfing the Web with a

Java-enabled browser is a more risky activity than surfing the Web in the days before Java.

It seems unlikely that all users of Java-enabled browsers will consider the security implications of surfing a site *before each Web page access*. If the new executable-content paradigm is going to work, all security concerns should be addressed in the language of the content itself. That way, users will not need to worry about security. Java's designers took this task to heart. One of their fundamental concerns was making the use of Java transparent, automatic, and above all safe. As a result, Java was developed with key security issues in mind.

It is clear that the Java development environment attempts to address the security problems introduced by the idea of dynamically download-ing and running external, untrusted code. To what extent Java succeeds in this task is a subject of debate. Security concerns have always been one of the major technical stumbling blocks to achieving safe executable content on the Web. Java took these concerns seriously and made a good effort to protect Web users. In this chapter we present the current Java security model and discuss how it mitigates some of the risks that applets introduce.

Potential Threats

Java applets are far more powerful than the usual HTML code served up on the Web. If not restricted by applet-security measures, Java is a complete and powerful programming language capable of sending information over the network; reading, altering, or deleting files; using system resources, and so on. This is powerful stuff, and in the hands of a malicious programmer (or even just a bad programmer), Java code could do some damage to a user's system. But people surfing the Web should not be burdened with such worries. Java should put these wor-ries to rest by providing an automatic security solution. Java should restrict itself such that the full power and potential of the Java language is not misused. After all, *who wants to run a Java applet that erases your hard disk?*

The design problem lies in the fact that programs running on personal computers usually have unlimited access to all of the resources of their machine. Most PC applications run as total system tyrants while they run. But if the Java applets you retrieve from the Web have been written by somebody else, you should not trust them to perform with integrity. Java code downloaded from the Net is automatically considered *untrusted* code. In order to ensure that untrusted code does nothing mischievous, it is important to limit what that untrusted code can do. Of course, completely limiting access to a system defeats the purpose of having executable content in the first place. After all, *who wants to run a program that is not allowed to do anything?*

Somehow these two extremes need to be balanced. Java applets need enough power to do some things, and sufficient restrictions that they can't do others. The solution is controlling access to system resources carefully. This is what the Java security model aims to do.

Before we talk about the internals of the Java security model, it is important to discuss the potential problems raised by executable content. There are four basic categories of potential attacks Java applets could facilitate:

- attacks that modify the system
- attacks that deny legitimate use of the machine by hogging resources
- attacks that invade a user's privacy
- attacks that antagonize a user

Table 2.1 lists the four classes in order of severity. There will be a brief discussion of each in turn. Keep in mind that this list of attacks is meant only to give a flavor of the kinds of things possible. It is by no means a complete list.

Table 2.1 People who use Java are susceptible to four classes of security threats. These threats are listed in order of severity, starting with the most severe and ending with the merely antagonistic. Hostile applets are divided into two types. *Attack applets* implement system modification attacks. These are as serious as being hacked by a cracker. *Malicious applets* implement the three remaining less serious risk classes.

Threat class	Explanation and consequences	Java defense
System Modification	The most severe class of threats. Applets that implement such attacks are *attack applets*. Consequences of these threats: severe.	Strong
Invasion of Privacy	If you value your privacy, this threat class may be particularly odious. They are implemented by *malicious applets*. Include mail forging. Consequences of these threats: moderate.	Strong
Denial of Service	Also serious but not severely so, these attacks can bring a machine to a standstill. Also implemented by *malicious applets*. May require reboot. Consequences of these threats: moderate.	Weak
Antagonism	Merely annoying, this threat class is the most commonly encountered. Implemented by malicious applets. May require restart of browser. Consequences of these threats: light.	Weak

System Modification

Java is a very powerful programming language and with this power comes the potential for abuse. Most programming languages have the ability to modify data on the run time system. Java includes pre-defined classes with methods that can delete and otherwise modify files, modify memory, and even kill processes and threads. System modification attacks comprise the most critical risks. Java's designers have given much thought to preventing this class of attack.

In the most serious cases, system modification involves intrusion into the system itself. Like many parts of today's complex systems, Java can be misused as an avenue of attack. Given that crackers will use any tool available to compromise the security of a machine, special care must be taken to ensure that Java does not provide new ports of entry to a machine. That Java is designed to work on many different platforms makes this task that much more important. *

The good news is that using Java to break into a machine is not easy. The bad news is that such break-ins are certainly possible. This book refers to applets that implement system modification attacks as *attack applets*. Attack applets are a serious concern. In Chapter 3 you will see how several such attacks have been successfully applied in the laboratory. Patches have been developed that make these attacks impossible, but the threat of other sophisticated attacks remains.

With so many machines running mission critical applications, system modification attacks could lead to things like modified financial records in a database. This could lead to financial loss and corporate bankruptcy. Modified patient records could result in fatally incorrect treatment. Care must be taken not to expose critical systems to new lines of attack.

---

* The implication here is that a Java-based attack that is successful on one platform, say, Solaris machines, will be just as successful on Windows-NT machines. Never before have cross-platform attacks been such a distinct possibility.

Crackers flock to the latest and greatest vulnerabilities. It is important that Java not become a cracking tool.

Invasion of Privacy

A second general type of attack involves disclosing information about a user or host machine that should not be publicized. Some files are meant to be kept confidential. For example, on UNIX machines, if someone gains access to the **/etc/passwd** file (which contains usernames and encrypted passwords) he or she could mount a password-cracking attack. A successful cracking attack is a complete invasion of a machine.

Sensitive information of other sorts can also be leaked from a system. Consider the implications of an unscrupulous company being able to steal the secret business plans of a competitor through corporate espionage. Or, if you are not a corporate user, consider your private e-mail correspondence or your financial records being made public. If such confidential information is mailed or otherwise transferred off a system, the act can be called an invasion of privacy.

Most modern workstations include sound capability. This opens up users to a new kind of eavesdropping. If an attacker can gain control of the microphone, then it is possible to listen in on the area immediately surrounding the workstation. More subtle eavesdropping includes monitoring process tables and file access. A Web-based version of eavesdropping might include keeping track of which links a user follows.

Forging mail could also be construed as a kind of invasion of privacy attack. If an outsider can gain enough information to successfully forge mail that appears to be from you, then you are exposed to a large number of serious risks. As is discussed in Chapter 4, Java makes the standard mail-forging attack a much more serious threat.

Java successfully defends against some of these attacks. For example, file I/O is very closely guarded. However, this good feature is countered by the fact that applets always have a channel open back to their original host server. Should the applet somehow dig up some information, it would be very easy to send that information back to the original host server. Non–file-related members of the invasion of privacy class (such as mail forging) are harder to defend against. Short of disabling a client's ports, the mail forging attack is likely to remain a threat.

Denial of Service

Denial of service attacks make system resources unavailable. They occur when a process allocates more than the standard allotment of resources, essentially hogging the machine. There are many sub-categories of denial of service attacks. Some examples include:

- completely filling a file system
- using up all available file pointers
- allocating all of a system's memory
- creating thousands of windows, effectively denying access to the output screen or window event queue
- using all of the machine's cycles (CPU time) by creating many high-priority threads

Though denial of service attacks are a real concern, Java's designers were not able to protect users from this class of attacks.

There is some debate over the relative importance of stopping denial of service attacks. In most cases, denial of service is more closely related to the class of annoyance attacks than to anything else. This is because recovering from a denial of service attack is usually not difficult. But some computer systems perform very important, even mission-critical tasks. Denial of service to such a machine could be very serious. Consider the mayhem that would erupt should a malicious program clog up the machines running the stock market. Losses could be staggering.

Denial of service attacks are by far the most commonly encountered Java security concern. Implementing such an attack is not hard, but stopping one is. Malicious applets, the subject of Chapter 4, often make use of denial of service attacks. Unfortunately, the current security model does not offer a good solution to the denial of service problem. Planned enhancements to the Java security model promise to lessen the threat posed by denial of service attacks.

Antagonism

Less odious, but still of some concern, are attacks that merely antagonize or annoy a user. Playing unwanted sound files through a speaker or displaying obscene pictures on a monitor are two examples. Sometimes seemingly antagonistic attacks may be the result of simple programming errors. Chapter 4 contains some examples of antagonistic malicious applets.

Some denial of service attacks could be classified as merely antagonistic. A window-popping attack, for example, can be reduced to an annoyance depending on the window manager in use. Judging the severity and category of a particular attack is always a subjective and context-sensitive problem. This is no reason to pretend that such categories do not exist. In order to more thoroughly understand the risks associated with executable content (hence, Java applets), these attacks need to be considered.

What Applets Can't Do

Java applications do not have the same security implications as applets. Thus with an application, it is possible to read and write files, communicate with devices, connect to sockets, and so on. But applets are different. Clearly Java applets need to be stopped from doing some of these things. Applet access to the more powerful features of Java must be properly restricted.

The most important Java security issues crop up when we talk about applets. Applets are Java's version of executable content. There are many things that Java applets should not be allowed to do, and many resources to which Java applets should have only restricted access. The Java security model imposes these restrictions.

Applets can be related to the traditional client/server model in a straightforward manner: the Web server is the applet's server. It sends the applet to the client machine. The client is the machine on which the applet eventually runs. That means when you are surfing the Web and come across an applet, your machine is the client. This terminology is useful for explaining what applets are not allowed to do.

If an applet has been loaded across the network, it is not allowed to:

- read files on the client file system
- write files to the client file system
- delete files on the client file system, either by using the **File.delete()** method or by calling system-level **rm** or **del** commands
- rename files on the client file system, either by using the **File.renameTo()** method or by calling system-level **mv** or **rename** commands
- create a directory on the client file system, either by using the **File.mkdirs()** methods, or by calling the system-level **mkdir** command
- list the contents of a directory
- check to see whether a file exists
- obtain information about a file, including size, type, and modification time stamp
- create a network connection to any computer other than the host from which it originated
- listen for or accept network connections on any port on the client system
- create a top-level window without an *untrusted window* banner
- obtain the user's username or home directory name through any means including trying to read the system properties: **user.name**, **user.home**, **user.dir**, **java.home**, and **java.class.path**
- define any system properties

- run any program on the client system using the **Runtime.exec()** methods
- make the Java interpreter exit, using either **System.exit()** or **Runtime.exit()**
- load dynamic libraries on the client system using the **load()** or **loadLibrary()** methods of the **Runtime** or **System** classes
- create or manipulate any thread that is not part of the same **ThreadGroup** as the applet
- create a **ClassLoader**
- create a **SecurityManager**
- specify any network control functions, including **ContentHandlerFactory**, **SocketImplFactory**, or **URLStreamHandlerFactory**
- define classes that are part of packages on the client system

Java applets are executed by Web browsers with embedded Java interpreters (VMs) and run time class libraries. Applets are downloaded by the browser and then interpreted by the built-in VM on the machine running the browser. The security of the system depends on these parts of the model: the Java language itself, the run time class libraries, and the security manager of the browser. The next section examines how the Java compiler and run time system restrict the creation and distribution of malicious code.

A Three-Pronged Defense

In addition to many safety-related characteristics of the Java language, Java security relies on three prongs of defense.* The next three sections are

---

* Before nailing down the terminology for this book, we originally referred to the Java security model as a "three-layer" defense. Though such a label is commonly encountered in the Java security literature, it is misleading. The layer terminology implies that if an applet penetrates the first "layer," two layers are left to set things straight. Actually, if any of the three prongs is exploited, the entire security system breaks. That is why throughout this book, we refer to the three parts of the Java security model as prongs.

each devoted to one prong: the *Byte Code Verifier*, the *Class Loader*, and the *Security Manager*. Each of these prongs depends in some way on the others. For the security model to function properly, each part must do its job flawlessly. Between them, the three prongs perform load and run time checks in order to restrict file system and network access (as well as restricting access to browser internals). Figure 2.1 shows how the three prongs of defense fit into the Java framework.

The Byte Code Verifier

Recall that when a Java program is compiled, it compiles down to platform-independent Java byte code. As can be seen in Figure 2.2, Java byte code is *verified* before it can run. This verification scheme is meant to ensure

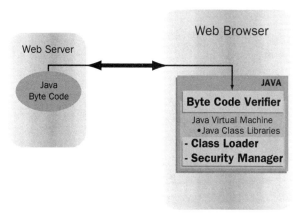

Figure 2.1 The three parts of the Java Security model are the byte code Verifier, the Class Loader, and the Security Manager. The Class Loader and the Security Manager are defined in the JDK class libraries.

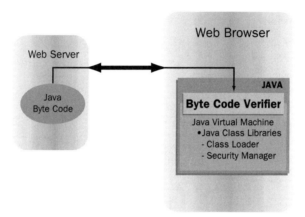

Figure 2.2 The byte code Verifier ensures that byte code plays by the rules. It acts as insurance against malicious compilers and is the first prong of defense in the Java security model.

that the byte code, which may or may not have been created by a Java compiler, plays by the rules. After all, byte code could well have been created by a "hostile compiler" that assembled byte code meant to crash the Java VM [Sun Microsystems, 1995]. Verifying byte code is one way in which Java automatically checks *untrusted* code before it is allowed to run

The Verifier checks byte code at a number of different levels. The simplest test makes sure that the format of a code fragment is correct. On a less basic level, a built-in theorem prover is applied to each code fragment. The theorem prover helps to make sure that byte code does not forge pointers, violate access restrictions, or access objects using incorrect type information. The verification process, in concert with the security features built into the language and checked by the compiler, helps to establish a base set of security guarantees.*

The Verifier reconstructs type state information by looking through the byte code. The types of all parameters of all byte code instructions must be checked. A key assumption the Verifier makes is that byte code may have come from an untrusted source. Because of this possibility, the Verifier provides a first line of defense against external code that may try to break the interpreter. Only code that passes the Verifier's tests will be run.

The Verifier checks a number of important properties. Once byte code passes through verification, the following things are guaranteed:

- Stacks will not be overflowed or underflowed. Overflowing stacks is a common attack that has led to several of the most notorious security vulnerabilities. The Internet worm used stack overflow as part of its arsenal [Spafford, 1989].
- Byte code instructions all have parameters of the correct type. For example, **InputStreams** are always used as **InputStreams** and nothing else.
- No illegal data conversions (casts) occur. For example, treating an integer as a pointer is not allowed.
- Private, public, and protected class accesses are legal. In other words, no access to restricted interfaces will be attempted.
- All register accesses and stores are valid.

---

* In Chapter 5, we will address this "dual nature" of the security model. Is it true that the Verifier allows only what the compiler allows? Or is the set of things that byte code can do larger than the set of things that should be possible to do in Java? The latter seems to be the case. In fact, we know of at least one instance in which it is possible to do something in byte code that it is not possible to do in Java source.

Computer scientists refer to the meaning of a language as its *semantics*, and the structure of a language is its *syntax*. When you are thinking about what a language can do, it is useful to talk about semantics. The semantics of the Java language provide much of Java's built-in security. It is critical that the semantics of Java be enforced in each and every Java program. Byte code is designed to contain enough symbolic information that safety verification (double checking the compiler-enforced safety rules) can occur. Byte code specifies the methods of a class as a set of Java Virtual Machine instructions. These instructions must pass a battery of tests before they can be run.

Class Files and Byte Code When Java source code is compiled, the results of the compilation are put into files ending with the **.class** extension. Java class files are made up of streams of 8-bit bytes. Larger values requiring 16 or 32 bits are composed of multiple 8-bit bytes. Class files contain several pieces of information in a particular format. Included in a class file are:

- a magic constant
- major and minor version information
- the constant pool (a heterogeneous array composed of five primitive types)
- information about the class (name, superclass, etc.)
- information about the fields and methods in the class
- debugging information

[Sun Microsystems, 1996b; Sun Microsystems, 1996c]

The byte code inside a **.class** file is made up of instructions that can be divided into several categories. Called *opcodes*, byte code instructions implement:

- pushing constants onto the stack
- accessing and modifying the value of a VM register

- accessing arrays
- manipulating the stack
- arithmetic instructions
- logic instructions
- conversion instructions
- control transfer
- function return
- manipulating object fields
- invoking methods
- creating objects
- type casting

Since it exists at the level of the VM, Java byte code is very similar to assembly language. Each line of byte code is a one-byte *opcode* followed by zero or more bytes of operand information. All instructions (with the exception of two table lookup instructions) are of fixed length.

Considered one level above the nitty-gritty level, class verification (of which byte code verification is a crucial step) occurs in four passes:

1. Ensure that the class file is in the proper format. This includes checking the magic number and making sure that all attributes are of the right length. The byte code cannot be too short or too long, and the constant pool is able to be parsed.
2. Verify anything that can be done without looking at the byte code. This includes the following checks:

    a. **final** classes cannot be sub-classed or overridden

    b. every class must have a superclass

    c. the constant pool must satisfy more stringent constraints

    d. all field references and method references in the constant pool must have legal names, legal classes, and a legal type signature

3. Verify the byte code using data-flow analysis. At any given point in the byte code program, no matter how that point is reached, all of the following must hold:

    a. the stack is always the same size

    b. register access is checked for proper value type

    c. methods have appropriate arguments

    d. fields are modified with values of the appropriate type

    e. all opcodes have proper type arguments on the stack and in the registers

(See [Sun Microsystems, 1996c]).

4. Load in the definition of any class that is required but not yet loaded. Verify that the currently executing class is allowed to reference the newly-loaded class. After performing its duties, pass four can re-write an opcode instruction with a specially-tagged quick version for later run time speed. The way this quick tagging is implemented turns out to be important. (See Chapter 3.)

In addition to the four verification steps above, there are some run time checks that occur during execution while a class is actually running. For example, whenever an instruction calls a method, or modifies a field, the run time checks ensure that the method or field exists, check the call for the proper form, and check the executing method for access privilege.

Checking for Run Time Exceptions   The main benefit that the Verifier provides is that the interpreter runs faster. The Verifier removes much of the checking that the interpreter would otherwise need to do. For example, the interpreter can ignore operand type checking and stack overflow checking since it has already been done. The interpreter then runs at full speed.

The Java Run Time and the Verifier   The byte code Verifier acts as the primary gatekeeper in the Java security model. It ensures that each piece of byte code downloaded from the outside plays by the rules.* That way, the Java VM can interpret byte code that may not have been created by a Java compiler.

In order for the Verifier to succeed in its role as gatekeeper, the Java run time system must be correctly implemented. Bugs in the run time system will make byte code verification useless. It appears that the Java run time from Sun Microsystems is mostly correct (see Chapter 3). This notion of run time correctness is complicated by the fact that rights to create and distribute Java run time systems have been granted to several companies (including Netscape, Symantec, Borland, and Microsoft).

There are currently plans to create validation and verification test suites for the entire Java development environment. However, these test suites have neither been completely developed nor verified by outside experts. It is especially critical to verify any third-party Java environment to ensure that it properly implements the Java run time. Without a guarantee of bug-free run time, Java security falls to pieces. Java users should think carefully about the Java run time product that they use.

The Applet Class Loader

The second security defense is the Java Applet Class Loader. Recall that all Java objects belong to classes. The Applet Class Loader determines when and how an applet can add classes to a running Java environment. Part of its job is to make sure that important parts of the Java run time environment are not replaced by code that an applet tries to install.

In general, a running Java environment can have many Class Loaders active, each defining its own *name space*. Name spaces allow Java classes to be separated into distinct kinds according to where they originate (see Figure 2.3). The Applet Class Loader, which is typically

---

* Not all security rules can be checked during static verification. Those that can't be checked in advance are checked during run time.

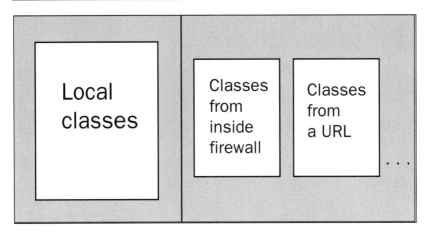

Figure 2.3 The Java environment is a dynamic environment in which classes both arrive and depart. The Class Loader divides classes that it loads into several distinct name spaces according to where the classes came from. Local classes are kept distinct from classes loaded from other machines. Furthermore, these outside classes are protected from each other.

supplied by the browser vendor, loads all applets and the classes they reference. When an applet loads across the network, the Applet Class Loader receives the binary data and *instantiates* it as a new class. Under normal operation, applets are forbidden to install a new Class Loader, so the Applet Class Loader is the only game in town.

A complete Java application (such as the Java interpreter built in to Netscape or Internet Explorer) can, however, set up its own Class Loader. Sun Microsystems provides a template Class Loader module as part of the Java Developers Kit. If an applet could somehow install a Class Loader, the applet would be free to define its own name space. This would allow an attack applet to breach security (see Chapter 3). If you are writing an application or built-in extension that defines its own Class Loader, you should be very careful to follow the rules; otherwise your Class Loader will almost certainly introduce a security hole. One criticism often raised against the Java security model is that because of the presence of objects like application-definable Class Loaders, the security model is too distributed and lacks central control.

The Applet Class Loader installs each applet in a separate name space. This means that each applet sees its own classes and all of the classes in the standard Java library API, but it doesn't see classes belonging to other applets. Hiding applets from each other in this way has two advantages. It allows multiple applets to define classes with the same name without ill effect. Applet writers don't have to worry about name collisions. It also makes it harder, though not impossible, for applets to team up.

Internally, the Java Virtual Machine tags each class with the Class Loader that installed it. This allows the VM to differentiate between a class that belongs to an applet and a class that was loaded from the local disk. The Class Loader label on classes is used in several places in the VM to make decisions about security. You can think of it as an ownership tag that tells the VM to whom each class belongs.

When a class is imported from the network, the Applet Class Loader places it into a private name space labeled with information about its origin. Whenever one class tries to reference another, the Applet Class Loader follows a particular order of search. The first place it looks for a class is in the local name space where built-in classes live. If there is no such name in the local space, the Applet Class Loader widens the search to include the name space of the class making the reference. In addition, the Applet Class Loader allows local classes to reference classes outside the local name space by specifying an explicit reference to an outside name space (including, say, the URL). Similarly, the Applet Class Loader allows external classes to reference other external name spaces only explicitly, and only if the methods they are referencing have been declared **public**.

Because the Applet Class Loader searches for built-in classes first, it prevents imported classes from pretending to be built-in classes (something known as "spoofing"). This policy prevents such things as applets redefining file I/O operations to gain unrestricted access to the file system. Clearly, the point is to protect fundamental primitives from outside corruption.

The Applet Class Loader puts all applets from a particular source in the same name space. This means that they can reference each others' methods. A source is defined as a particular directory on a particular Web server.

Each Java class begins as source code. This is then compiled into byte code and distributed to machines anywhere on the Net. A java-enabled browser automatically downloads a class when it encounters the **<APPLET>** tag in an HTML document. The Verifier examines the byte code of a class file to ensure that it follows Java's strict safety rules. The Java VM interprets byte code declared safe by the Verifier. The Java specification allows classes to be unloaded when they are no longer needed, but current Java implementations never unload classes.

The Java Security Manager

The third prong of the Java security model is the Java Security Manager.[*] This part of the security model restricts the ways an applet uses visible interfaces. The Security Manager implements a good portion of the entire security model.

The Security Manager is a single module that performs run time checks on dangerous methods. Code in the Java library consults the Security Manager whenever a potentially dangerous operation is attempted. The Security Manager is given a chance to veto the operation by generating a Security Exception. Decisions made by the Security

---

[*] The Security Manager was added to the JDK during the move from alpha to beta release. It was specifically designed to increase security.

Manager take into account which Class Loader installed the requesting class. Obviously, built-in classes are given more privilege than classes loaded across the Net.

The Security Manager is completely customizable (through subclassing), though applets are not allowed to define Security Managers. A default Security Manager is provided (like the Class Loader) as a template from Sun Microsystems. Each Java-enabled application fills in the template to meet security requirements for the application. The Java run time library is written so that all access requests are referred to the Security Manager. Access requests are used for thread access, OS access, network access, and Java component access.

The Security Manager has the following duties:

- Preventing installation of new Class Loaders. The Class Loader's job is to keep the name spaces properly organized. Because things like file I/O permission will depend on whether or not a class is local, the Class Loader has an important job. It must not be subject to *spoofing*.
- Protecting threads and thread groups from each other. (Unfortunately, the current implementation of this piece of policy does not function properly. Some malicious applets, discussed in Chapter 4, have been written to take advantage of this.)
- Controlling the creation of OS programs.
- Controlling access to OS processes.
- Controlling file system operations such as **read** and **write**. Access to local files is strictly controlled.
- Controlling socket operations such as **connect** and **accept**.
- Controlling access to Java packages (or groups of classes).

The Security Manager can be customized. The **appletviewer**, part of the Java Developers Kit, reads a configuration file with several user-determined security options. These configuration files declare that low-level details, such as "**myfile.txt** should be writable by applets."

Each Java-enabled browser uses its own version of the Security Manager to restrict file I/O by foreign applets. This prevents applets from processing data on a user's machine, and imposes a large, but important, blockade on what applets can do today.

The job of the Security Manager will be affected by many of the future plans for Java security (see Chapter 6). One of the most promising new technologies will allow applets to be digitally *signed* using advanced encryption algorithms. Using encryption-based authentication methods, the Security Manager could set up much more sophisticated rules for trusted, partially-trusted, and untrusted applets. It is likely that organizations will be set up to approve applets after thoroughly checking them. When approved, these applets could be digitally signed with a stamp of approval. Such digital signing will certainly improve the Java security model.

Different Classes of Security

As Figure 2.4 shows, there are three possible paths that byte code can take through the Java security model. The path that is taken is determined by the origin of the byte code. Built-in byte code from the distribution (off the local disk) is allowed to bypass the verification stage. This means that built-in classes are assumed to be both correct and well-behaved. All other byte code classes must pass through the strict security checks.

Built-in Classes: The Privileged Class

The JDK includes a class library that makes Java as powerful as it is. Since this code is part of Java itself, it is considered trustworthy. The fact that built-in Java classes bypass security measures has many implications. The system makes sense when you consider that this code is part of the interpreter. If the interpreter is loaded before the Verifier, there is no choice but to consider the built-in Java classes trustworthy.

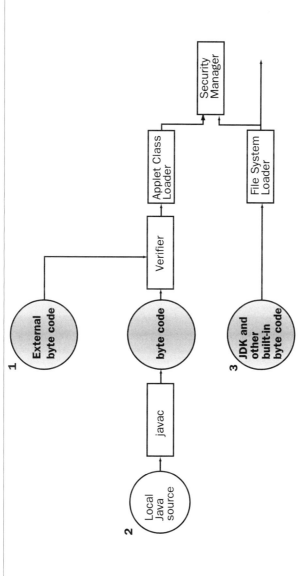

Figure 2.4 There are three possible paths that Java byte code may follow through the security model. The path chosen depends on where the byte code originates. External byte code (loaded across the network) (1) must be verified, and is subject to the Class Loader and the Security Manager. Locally developed byte code (2) is subject to the same checks (unless it is in the CLASSPATH). Local Java source also gets checked during compilation by the javac compiler. Byte code from the JDK distribution (and other class collections in the CLASSPATH) (3) does not pass through the Verifier, and may be subject to further optional security checks.

49

It is not just JDK classes that can bypass security. Any class stored on the local file system and made part of the local approved set of classes will be considered a built-in class. Such classes are, however, only subject to automatic loading if they are placed in one of the sub-directories in the CLASSPATH. Making a change to the CLASSPATH, or placing a new class in one of these sub-directories is tantamount to making a fundamental change in your security policy. A good example of classes given built-in status is the set of class files included with Netscape Navigator: **moz2_0.zip** or **moz3_0.zip**, depending on the version of the browser.

It is essential that you never install classes of unknown origin as built-in classes by putting them in the CLASSPATH. Since the security checks are bypassed for this kind of byte code, granting such classes built-in status is very dangerous. Install only vendor-supplied classes as built-in classes.

The file system loader shown in Figure 2.4 sets up the name space for built-in classes. This name space is special. The local name space is exclusively reserved for built-in classes. This helps protect built-in classes (including essential things like the Security Manager) from spoofing by outside classes.

Built-in classes may or may not be subjected to the Security Manager, depending on the policy of the site. Vendor-supplied classes often require unhindered access to system resources. Classes like the **ClassLoader** must be trusted in order to bootstrap the system.

Non–built-in Classes: The Unwashed Masses

All classes not considered built-in are subject to more strict security checks. Paths (1) and (2) of Figure 2.4 both apply to non–built-in classes. Classes in path (1) include all applets loaded from the network. Classes in path (2) include all applets loaded locally, but not specified in the CLASSPATH. It is not possible to stress heavily enough how important it is to consider carefully which classes you grant built-in status. If you install a Java class in your CLASSPATH it will no longer be subject to security checks. Only completely trusted code should be given this privilege.

Type Safety

The Java language is designed to enforce *type safety*. This means that programs are prevented from accessing memory in inappropriate ways. More specifically, every piece of memory is part of some Java object. Each object has some *class*. For example, a calendar-management applet might use classes like **Date**, **Appointment**, **Alarm**, and **GroupCalendar**. Each class defines both a set of objects and operations to be performed on the objects of that class. In our calendar management example, the **Alarm** class might define a **turnOn** operation, but the **Date** class would neither need nor allow **turnOn**. Type safety means that a program cannot perform an operation on an object unless that operation is valid for that object.

Why Type Safety Matters

Type safety is the most essential element of Java's security. To understand why, consider the following slightly contrived example. A calendar-management applet defines a class called **Alarm**. This class is represented in memory as shown in Figure 2.5. **Alarm** defines an operation **turnOn** which sets the first field to **true**. The Java run time library defines another class called **Applet**, whose memory layout is also shown in Figure 2.5. Note that the first field of **Applet** is **fileAccessAllowed**, which determines whether or not the applet is allowed access to files on the hard disk.

Suppose a program tried to apply the **turnOn** operation to an **Applet** object. If the operation was allowed to go ahead, it would do what **turnOn** was supposed to do, and set the first field of the object to **true**. Since the object was really in the **Applet** class, setting the first field

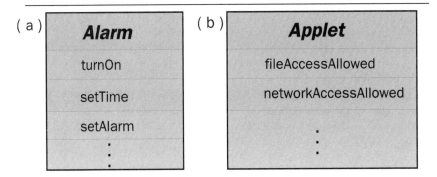

Figure 2.5 Memory representations of two classes: (a) Alarm; (b) Applet.

to **true** allows the applet to access the hard disk. The applet would then be allowed (incorrectly) to delete files.

This example shows what can go wrong if type safety is violated. In our experience, every type safety violation has created an opportunity for an untrusted applet to break out of Java's security restrictions. Given the importance of type safety, the next section will explain Java's strategy for ensuring type safety.

How Java Enforces Type Safety

Every Java object is stored in some region of the computer's memory. Java labels every object by putting a *class tag* next to the object. One simple way to enforce type safety is to check the class tag of the object before every operation on the object. This will help make sure the object's class allows the operation. This approach is called *dynamic type checking*.

Though dynamic type checking works, it is inefficient. The more time a system spends checking class tags, the more slowly programs run. To improve performance, Java uses *static type checking*. Java looks at the program before it is run, and carefully determines which way the tag checking operations will come out. This is more complicated, but more efficient than dynamic type checking. If Java can figure out that a particular tag checking operation will always succeed, then there is no reason to do it more than once. The check can safely be removed, speeding up the program.

The designers of Java carefully crafted the Java language and byte code formats to facilitate static type checking. The byte code Verifier is a very effective static type checker, eliminating almost all of the tag checking operations from Java programs. The result is a type safe program that runs quite efficiently.

Type Confusion

There is only one problem with Java's static type checking strategy: it's complicated. Though Java's designers obviously got the overall strategy right, there are a great many details that have to be perfect for type safety to be enforced. An error in any of these details would be a tiny but crucial hole in Java's type safety enforcement dike.

A clever cracker who finds such a hole can launch a type confusion attack. Such an attacker could write a Java applet designed to trigger a tiny type enforcement error. The attacker could then create a situation like our **Alarm/Applet** example in which the program has one kind of object but Java thinks that object has some other kind. As in the example, this seemingly harmless confusion can be exploited to breach Java's security. There are several real-life type confusion attacks discussed in Chapter 3.

Browser-specific Security Rules

As we noted above, two of the fundamental pieces of the Java security model, the Class Loader and the Security Manager, are meant to be defined by the browser vendor through subclassing. The rules browsers enforce make up the security policy defined by a particular vendor. Ultimately, Netscape could decide to implement different rules than Microsoft.

Of course, every browser's security implementation depends entirely on the rest of the security model being properly defined. Critical pieces of the Java environment directly affecting security include the Java VM, and the built-in libraries of the JDK. If any of these pieces have errors, the entire security system will break, regardless of which vendor does the other parts.

Netscape Navigator and Microsoft Internet Explorer

All Netscape Navigator versions subsequent to 2.0 are Java enabled. All Microsoft Internet Explorer versions subsequent to 3.0 also include Java. It is, however, very easy to disable Java in both kinds of browsers (see Chapter 4). There is a toggle switch for the entire Java environment. In both Netscape and Internet Explorer, Java is enabled by default.

The two browsers' security policies are, at the present time, exactly the same. Both are somewhat strict. The following rules apply to all applets running under Netscape and Internet Explorer:

- Applets cannot read or write files locally.
- Applets cannot open a network connection to any machine other than the applet's origin host.
- Applets can read only nine system properties. This allows an applet to access information such as the vendor who created the Java VM, the VM version number, the file separation character (either \ or /), the character used to separate lines, and so on. Applets are not permitted to read any other system properties.
- If an applet is loaded using the **file:** URL, and it does not reside in a directory in CLASSPATH, it is loaded by the Applet Class Loader.

There is no reason that all future browser vendors will choose to implement similar security policies. That two major vendors now do so is probably an artifact of Java's relative youth. Once browsers begin to implement different policies, security issues will become more complex.

The Fundamental Tradeoff

In Chapter 1, it was pointed out that there is no such thing as 100% security. Where security is concerned, there is a fundamental tradeoff between power (functionality) and security. Java attempts to be both powerful and secure. Java is breaking new ground in computer security by trying to manage complex security issues proactively. Despite such efforts, some flaws in the model still need to be addressed.

Functionality and security will always exist in an inverse relationship. Currently, Net users choose functionality over security. Java designers are attempting to increase security without paying too high a price in functionality.

Is There Really a Java Security Policy?

The Java Security model is comprised of three major components: the byte code Verifier, the Class Loader, and the Security Manager. Each of these components must work properly in order for Java to perform in a secure fashion. Java applications, including Java-enabled Web browsers, are allowed to customize two of the fundamental portions of the security model to suit their needs (the Class Loader and the Security Manager). This makes the security model much more distributed than many computer security experts would like [Badger and Kohli, 1995; Sams.net, 1996]. In the end, a great deal of faith is placed in the ability of a Java-enabled Web browser to ensure that applets remain properly contained. Bugs in the system will compromise the entire security model.

There is no formal, high-level security model in Java. Instead, the security policy is derived from a collection of low-level detail checking. This is difficult because without a formal model it is impossible to say what *secure* means. With no standardized model, each vendor is free to reinvent the term secure. In addition, no particular implementation can be verified.

The Java run time system is large (upwards of 28,000 lines of code, not including the VM). This raises important security assurance questions. Generally speaking, programs as large and complex as that are extremely hard to verify. It is common knowledge that buggy software causes many security vulnerabilities [Garfinkle and Spafford, 1996]. There is no centralized authority ensuring Java's security code is bug free.

The Java security system has not yet been through a sufficient peer review. Fortunately, Sun Microsystems realizes the need and is currently working with third-party vendors to assess the security model. In the mean time, some security researchers (including the authors of this book) are spending a fair amount of effort trying to find its weaknesses. The next chapter discusses some of the problems researchers have found and what Java vendors are doing to address them.

Chapter 3

Serious Holes
in the Security Model
Creating attack applets in the lab

There is a tightrope to walk in this chapter. You should understand the problems encountered with Java, so you will know how things can go wrong. But it is not the intent of this book to give the bad guys a manual for invading your computer. Although we will discuss Java security problems, we hope you'll forgive the omission of details necessary to exploit these problems.

Sun Microsystems and the rest of the Java industry have been hyping Java as completely secure [Sun Microsystems, 1995]. This is no surprise. They have a lot to gain if you believe them. It's true that Sun Microsystems, Netscape, and Microsoft have gone to great lengths to make their Java implementations as secure as possible. That's all well and good, but you don't want effort—you want results. Is Java safe enough to use?

This chapter examines all of the serious security flaws that have been found in Java so far. By *serious* we mean attacks based on these flaws could go beyond annoyance. These attacks could corrupt data on your hard disk, reveal your private data to third parties, or infect your machine with a virus. By exploiting some of the vulnerabilities discussed here, a cracker could attain the ultimate cracker goal—complete control of your machine.

By the time this book reaches you, all of these problems will have been fixed in the latest Java-enabled browsers. That means if you're using an up-to-date version of your favorite browser, these specific problems won't affect you. If you want to make sure that the browser you're using is up to date, take a look at this book's Web site (**http://www .rstcorp.com/java-security.html**).

Though these specific attacks are not likely to be your problem since they have been fixed, they indicate what sorts of things can go wrong, and what the consequences are when things do go wrong. If more Java security problems are found in the future, they're likely to be similar to the ones presented here.

Most of these problems were trivial to fix once they were discovered. Removing security bugs is like removing needles from a haystack: it's hard to find the needles, but they're easy to remove once you know where they are. To push the analogy a bit: it's obviously much better to find the needles before they stick you. This principle motivates our Java security research.

Attack Applets

It is important to reemphasize that the attacks described in this chapter are not hypothetical. Each of the attacks described in this chapter has been implemented by the Safe Internet Programming team (SIP) at Princeton University. Each was successfully used to break into a machine in the team's laboratory. Naturally, the Princeton team did not release the resulting attack applets onto the Net.

Attack applets are the most dangerous kind of hostile applets. They do more than simply annoy or deny service. The end result of an attack applet is the same as being hacked by a cracker. Your system is wide-open for unauthorized access.

According to the CERT Coordination Center, an organization that keeps track of computer security violations on the Internet, there have been no confirmed reports of loss due to the attacks described in this chapter. There are, however, a few cases of attacks possibly carried out with applets. It is, of course, impossible to rule out the possibility of attacks that haven't been discovered, or that haven't been reported. The lack of reports indicates that the number of attacks, if any, has been small. Successfully implemented attack applets probably haven't occurred, but there can be no guarantee that one won't show up tomorrow. The danger is real enough that CERT recommends people disable Java when using particular versions of popular browsers [CERT, 1996a; CERT, 1996b]. The full text of these CERT alerts is included here as Appendix B.

What Applets Aren't Supposed to Do

Chapter 2 discussed the Java security model at length. Java's designers tried to ensure applets could not misbehave. For a concise listing of things that Java applets should not be allowed to do, see Chapter 2. It is also worth reading the "Frequently Asked Questions Applet Security" Web page served by Sun Microsystems (**http://java.javasoft.com/sfaq**) [Sun Microsystems, 1996a]. In order to provide concrete examples of Java security policies that work, Sun's Security FAQ page includes pointers to a number of applets that cannot get around Java security. The good news is that straightforward approaches to breaching security will fail. The bad news is that crackers usually don't give up after the straightforward approach fails. Fortunately, neither do security researchers.

It is always interesting to get an objective outsider's opinion about Java security. That is probably one of the reasons you are reading this book. Appendix A includes a hard copy of the Princeton Safe Internet Programming team's Java Security FAQ. An up-to-the-minute version of that FAQ can be found at **http://www.cs.princeton.edu/sip/ java-faq.html**. You may also reference this book's Web site at **http:// www.rstcorp.com/java-security.html**.

A History of Problems

To date, eight serious security problems have been discovered in implementations of Java. A brief chronology follows which describes each flaw. Later in this chapter these flaws will be discussed in more detail. Some of these flaws allow full system penetration. This means that an attacker could exploit them to do literally anything to your machine, including corrupting your data, reading your private data, injecting a virus, or leaving a trapdoor to re-enter your machine at will.

> *February 96: Drew Dean, Edward Felten, and Dan Wallach at Princeton discovered a flaw in Java's networking software, affecting Netscape Navigator 2.0. This flaw was postulated independently by Steve Gibbons. It could be exploited to launch security attacks on other machines on a private network. This flaw was fixed in Netscape Navigator 2.01. The resulting attack is called Jumping the Firewall. See page 62. This attack resulted in one of the two Java-related CERT alerts included in Appendix B [CERT, 1996a].*

> *March 96: David Hopwood at Oxford University found a flaw that allows an attack which tricks Java into treating the attacker's applet as trusted code. This flaw allowed full system penetration. It affected Netscape Navigator 2.01 and was fixed in Netscape Navigator 2.02. The resulting attack is called Slash and Burn. See page 69.*

> *March 96: The Princeton team (Dean, Felten and Wallach) found a bug in the Java byte code Verifier and a flaw in the class-loading*

mechanism. Together, these allowed full system penetration. This problem affected Netscape Navigator 2.01 and was fixed in Netscape Navigator 2.02. The resulting attack is called Applets Running Wild. See page 75. This attack resulted in the second of the two Java-related CERT alerts included in Appendix B [CERT, 1996b].

May 96: *Independent consultant Tom Cargill, working with the Princeton team (Dirk Balfanz, Dean, Felten, and Wallach) found a flaw in the implementation of the Java interpreter. This flaw allowed full system penetration. It affected Netscape Navigator 2.02 and Microsoft Internet Explorer 3.0β1, and was fixed in Navigator 3.0β3 and Explorer 3.0β2. The resulting attack is called Casting Caution to the Wind. See page 82.*

June 96: *Hopwood found another flaw in the interpreter that again allowed full system penetration. This flaw affected Netscape Navigator 3.0β3 and was fixed in Navigator 3.0β4. The resulting attack is called Tag-team Applets. See page 85.*

June 96: *Balfanz, Dean, and Felten found a flaw in Java's implementation of array types that allowed full system penetration. This flaw affected Netscape Navigator 3.0β5 and was fixed in Navigator 3.0β6. The resulting attack is called You're not my Type. See page 72.*

July 96: *Cargill, Balfanz, Dean, and Felten found another implementation flaw in the Java interpreter. This flaw allowed an attacker to mount some attacks on network services on other private-network machines. This flaw affected Netscape Navigator 3.0β5 and was fixed in Navigator 3.0β6. This attack is also called Casting Caution to the Wind. See page 82.*

August 96: *Balfanz and Felten found a flaw in Microsoft's Java implementation. The flaw allowed code in an attack applet to* *become a member of a security-critical Java package, thus gaining the ability to change various security parameters. This in turn gives the applet full access to the target machine's files and the network. This flaw affected Microsoft Internet Explorer 3.0β3 and was fixed in Explorer 3.0β4. The resulting attack is called Big Attacks Come in Small Packages. See page 88.*

The rest of this chapter will describe these flaws in more detail.

Jumping the Firewall

In the first problem, an attack applet launches network security attacks on other machines. This is something that an attacker could already do before Java came along. The twist is that by embedding the attack into an applet, the bad guy makes the attack come from the machine of an innocent bystander. Example: you're sitting at your desk, happily browsing the web, and without realizing it, your machine is trying to penetrate the security of a machine down the hall.

This kind of confusion is reason enough to use Java as the penetration vehicle, but the culprit has an even better reason for using Java. Many corporate networks protect themselves from Internet intrusion through the use of a firewall. (See Figure 3.1.) If your firewall is well configured, it prevents the mischievous cracker from making direct use of the network to probe the defenses of your machines. The firewall does this by blocking certain types of network traffic from entering the corporate network.

A Java applet, though, doesn't look suspicious to the most firewalls. Typical firewalls examine the type of packet, not the contents of the packet. For some firewalls, to block Java applet traffic, a system manager would have to block all Web traffic.* The fact that your browser

---

* Some firewalls are now beginning to screen for Java class files, but it is unlikely that they will always be successful. For more on applet-blocking firewalls, see Chapter 5.

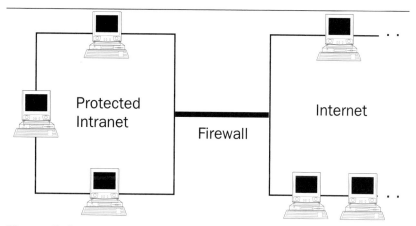

Figure 3.1 A firewall stands between your internal network and the rest of the Internet. It screens every packet of data coming across the network, allowing only certain kinds of packets through.

requested the applet makes the firewall's job that much trickier. If the applet can open network connections to other machines, it can connect from your machine to another machine behind the firewall. In the current case, the attack originates from the inside rather than the outside. Since the firewall only filters traffic coming from the outside, it is helpless to prevent this sort of attack. This is especially dangerous since many sites have strong firewall protection but almost no protection against attacks from the inside. In security circles, these sites are jokingly referred to as crunchy on the outside and chewy in the middle.

The people who designed Java-enabled browsers thought of the possibility of inside-the-network attacks, so they made a security rule to prevent it. The rule states:

> *An applet may not open a network connection, except back to the server from which it came.*

If enforced properly, this rule stops any network probing by applets. Netscape Navigator 2.0 did not enforce this rule properly. In order to understand what went wrong, you need to understand how machines are named on the Internet.

Internet Naming

Like people, machines on the Internet need to have names to identify them. Specific names help machines send messages across a network. These names are also numeric addresses. Because these numbers are often difficult to remember, there are two layers of network addressing in the Internet. The Internet Protocol (IP) uses only numeric addresses to communicate between machines. The Domain Name System (DNS) keeps track of how the user-friendly names correspond to the IP numbers used to establish a machine's low-level connections.

An IP address is just a number. For example, the Web server at JavaSoft has this numeric address: 11001110000110100011000001100100 in binary notation. IP addresses are often written in decimal form, which looks like 206.26.48.100. When the computers that make up the Internet talk to each other, they identify themselves with the numeric IP addresses. Computers deal naturally with numbers like this, but they are, to say the least, not very user-friendly.

The other sort of Internet name, DNS names, are made for people. They look like **java.sun.com**, or **cogsci.indiana.edu**. These names are made up of often intelligible words strung together with dots to separate them. DNS divides the world up into domains like **sun.com** (Sun Microsystems) and **cs.princeton.edu** (the Princeton University Computer Science department). Each domain corresponds to a single administrative entity. It is up to that entity to define names that end in its domain name. For example, the **cs.princeton.edu** domain is free to define names like **elvis.cs.princeton.edu**. Anybody can create their own domain by registering with an organization called InterNIC and paying a modest fee.

The owner of each domain is responsible for providing a DNS server machine that responds to queries about DNS names inside that domain. For example, if someone wants to know the IP address of **elvis.cs.princeton.edu**, they can ask the DNS server for **cs.princeton.edu**.

A single DNS name might refer to several IP addresses. There are two reasons for this. First, a machine might be connected to more than one network, with a separate IP address for each of its connections. Second, there might be several machines providing the same service. For example, **espnet.sportszone.com** might actually correspond to several machines, all providing identical services.

Sometimes several DNS addresses refer to the same machine, and hence the same IP address. For example, a company's Web server **www.rstcorp.com,** and its FTP server **ftp.rstcorp.com** might actually be the same machine. This makes sense because management might later want to move the two functions onto separate machines. Using two separate names allows them to keep this flexibility.

What Went Wrong: The Java DNS Security Bug

To enforce the rule that an applet can connect only to the server where it originated, the implementers of Java needed a way to check whether the machine an applet wanted to reach was the same as the machine that the applet came from. They did this as follows:

- Use DNS to translate the name of the Web server into a list of IP addresses.
- Use DNS to translate the name of the machine the applet wants to connect to into a list of IP addresses.
- Compare the two lists. If any address appears in both lists, declare the two machines are the same and allow the connection. If not, declare they are different and refuse the connection.

This way of using DNS to authenticate a host is illustrated in Figure 3.3. Though this approach seems good, it turns out to be too permissive.

The following scenario describes what can go wrong. Figure 3.2 shows the scenario visually.

> Imagine that a bad guy wants to attack a machine called **target** **.victim.org**, with the IP address 10.10.10.2. The bad guy sets up a Web server called **www.attacker.org**, with IP address 172.16.16.16; then he waits. An unsuspecting person, surfing the Web on **stooge.victim.org** (IP address 10.10.10.1), happens to visit the attacker's web site. The site contains a Java applet written by the attacker. The applet is downloaded to **stooge.victim.org** and run.

> The applet asks to create a network connection to **bogus.attacker.org**. Because that name is in the **attacker.org** domain, the attacker's DNS server is asked to provide an IP address for that machine and is free to provide any IP addresses it likes. The attacker's DNS server slyly returns the pair of addresses (10.10.10.2, 172.16.16.16). Because that list contains the address of the attacker's web server (172.16.16.16), Java erroneously concludes that **www.attacker.org** and **bogus.attacker.org** are really the same machine, so it allows the connection to go ahead.

> Unfortunately, after verifying the connection is allowed, Java connects to the first address on the list, 10.10.10.2, or **target.victim.org**. The attacker has achieved his goal: to connect to the target machine.

> What does the attacker do next? The attacker can systematically probe the defenses of the target machine, looking for weaknesses. Sophisticated tools such as SATAN even exist to automate this part [Farmer, 1996]. If the attacker finds a weakness, the victim could be in big trouble.

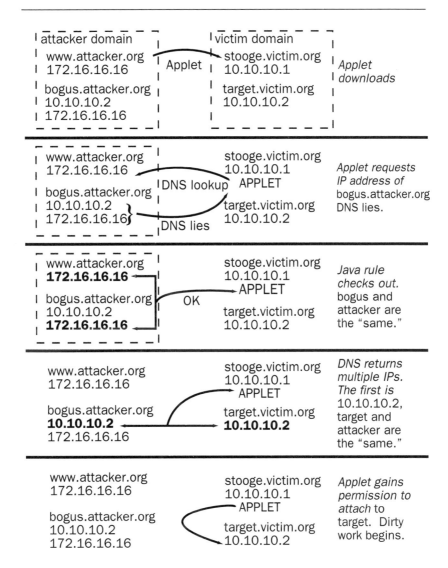

Figure 3.2 How the DNS security bug allows an applet to jump a site's firewall. The figure shows several different snapshots arranged in order of occurrence.

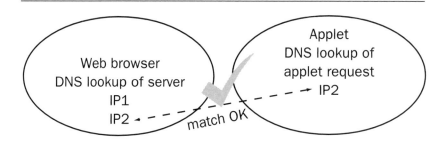

Figure 3.3 How Java originally used DNS to make sure that an applet attached only to the machine that served it.

The Fix

This problem was fixed by simply changing the criterion by which Java decides to allow a connection. The new approach is to store the IP address of the Web server, and allow a connection only to that IP address. This simple and complete solution is implemented in Netscape Navigator versions beginning with 2.01 and all Microsoft Internet Explorer versions.[*] It is no longer possible to jump the firewall with Java using the DNS bug. However, it is important to make sure that you are not using the unpatched Netscape 2.0.

The Reaction

The announcement of this flaw triggered a flurry of press reports, beginning with a story in *USA Today*. Reporters learned of the flaw from a brief message in the **comp.risks** forum. The discoverers of the attack were surprised to learn that many reporters monitor **comp.risks**.

It turned out that the existence of this flaw had been postulated independently by Steve Gibbons about four weeks before the

---

[*] Many software vendors still sell shrink-wrapped versions of Netscape Navigator 2.0, which includes the DNS bug. A key guideline for Java security is to use the latest patched versions of your Web browser. See Chapter 5.

announcement. Steve Gibbons had reported the bug to Sun Microsystems, but it was not fixed. After the *USA Today* article, Sun Microsystems and Netscape said they would fix the bug within days. It was fixed quite quickly.

The security researchers who uncovered the DNS attack were surprised to see that the press treated the news as a business story rather than as a technical story. This was probably a naive point of view. These days, technology reporting, even when discussing non-commercial technology, seems to be considered a branch of business reporting.

It was also surprising to see that many news organizations repeated a story that they had read elsewhere, without contacting the parties involved and apparently without reconfirming any of the facts! As usual when information is heard and then repeated, small inaccuracies creep in at each stage. It was sometimes possible to figure out who had copied the story from whom, by tracking small inconsistencies.

The *USA Today* story also triggered a blip in the stock market. Netscape's stock price dropped significantly on the day the story appeared. CNN and the Nightly Business Report attributed the drop to the announcement of this flaw, though there were other factors (for example, the expiration of the post-IPO embargo on insider sales) also driving down Netscape's stock that week. In any case, the stock bounced back when it became clear that the product was not irretrievably broken.

Slash and Burn

The second set of attacks involves Java code that passes itself off as belonging to the browser. Since code that comes with the browser is assumed to be safe (see Chapter 2), this fraud allows the malicious code access it would not ordinarily have. It could, for example, access files on the local disk.

In order to properly understand this attack, you need to understand how Java works. In particular, examine how Java accesses its own code on the browser's local disk.

Where Java Code Comes From

When a Java applet runs, many Java classes (pieces of Java code) are loaded and run. Some applet-related classes will be loaded by the applet, using the Web server. Other classes are part of the browser itself. Browser-related code is stored with the browser on the local disk. Netscape, for example, keeps its Java class files zipped up in an archive called **moz2_0.zip** or **moz3_0.zip**. When Netscape is installed, the class archive needs to be put somewhere special like **/usr/local/lib/netscape** on UNIX machines. Because the browser classes are part of the trusted browser program, they are given more privileges.

In general, Java treats code loaded from the local disk as trusted, and code loaded over the Net as untrusted. If an attacker can somehow get some malicious code loaded from the local disk, the attacker is home free.

From our discussion of the Java Class Loader in Chapter 2, we know that when Java needs to find a piece of code, say for a class **MyClass**, it first looks on the local disk for a file called **MyClass.class**. If Java fails to find an appropriate file on the local disk, then it tries to fetch the file from the Web server that originally provided the applet.

We've glossed over one key issue at this point: How does Java know what class to look for? The answer is that a class is only loaded when it is *mentioned* by another class already resident. This is called dynamic loading. The name of the mentioned class is stored in the Java code for the mentioning class.

Java classes have names like **security.book.chapter3**. When the Java system wants to look up a class on the disk, it translates the dots in the class name into backslashes. The name **security.book.chapter3** becomes

security\book\chapter3.* This transformed name is the file name used to search for the file on the local disk.

What Went Wrong: Dots and Slashes

If a bad guy wants to pass off a piece of code as trusted, two steps must be carried out: 1) getting the malicious code onto the victim's disk, and then 2) tricking the victim's browser into loading it.

The first part, getting code onto the victim's disk, isn't as hard as it sounds. For example, some machines have *public FTP* directories, where anybody can put a file. Alternatively, if the victim is using a shared, public machine, the attacker could get an account on that machine and put the file in that account's home directory.

Perhaps the most effective way to inject code is to take advantage of the browser's cache. Most Web browsers keep on-disk copies of files that they have recently accessed. This allows repeated accesses to the same Web documents without continually downloading the documents. Unfortunately, it also gives a malicious applet a way to get a file onto the victim's machine. The applet could load the file across the Net, pretending that it was an image or a sound file. Once this was done, the file would be on the victim's disk in the cache. If the applet knew how the browser organized its cache, it would know where on the victim's disk the file resided.

Once the file is on the victim's disk, the attacker tricks the victim's browser into loading the file. Since the browser only looks up class names in relation to the current directory, the attacker would have to place a file into the victim's working directory. File name lookup is relative because Java class names cannot start with a dot. Therefore, the translated name cannot start with a backslash.

---

* Actually, Java is capable of using either slashes or backslashes depending on the host's file system.

David Hopwood discovered that Java 1.0.1 and Netscape Navigator 2.01 erroneously allowed a class name to start with a backslash. Such a class name could reference any file on the system, not just those files associated with the browser. For example, a class named **\programs.browser.cache.file407** would be looked up on the local disk as **\programs\browser\cache\file407**.

This trick could be used to cause any file on the local disk to be loaded as Java code. Because code loaded from the local disk is trusted, it could proceed to illegally access the local system. This attack allows full system penetration—the bad guy can do anything at all on the victim's machine.

The Fix

This problem was fixed in Netscape Navigator 2.02, and in all versions of Microsoft Internet Explorer. The fix was simple: prohibit class names from starting with backslashes (or slashes, as the case may be). It is no longer possible to execute impostor code using the slash and burn attack.

You're Not My Type

As discussed in Chapter 2, the most common kind of serious security problem in Java involves type confusion. A type confusion attack confuses the Java system about the types of data objects it is manipulating.

The Java system treats objects as blocks of memory. Allocated memory contains the data fields of all objects, lined up one after the other. When a Java program has a reference to an object, what it really has internally is a pointer to the memory address storing the object. You can think of the pointer as tagged with a type that says what kind of object the pointer is pointing to.

As mentioned in Chapter 2, every aspect of Java security depends critically on the type-safety of the language. This means that if Java is going to be secure, it has to make sure that all pointers are properly tagged. That is, the tag must match the actual type of object that is being pointed to.

In a type-confusion attack, a malicious applet creates two pointers to the same object—with different type tags. When this happens, the Java system is in trouble. The applet can write into that memory address through one pointer, and read it through another pointer. The result is that the applet can bypass the typing rules of Java, completely undermining its security.

Figure 3.4 shows a type confusion attack at work. The applet has two pointers to the same memory, one pointer tagged with type **T** and one tagged with type **U**. Suppose that **T** and **U** are defined like this:

```
class T {
      SecurityManager x;
}
```

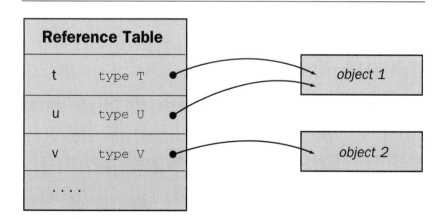

Figure 3.4 Type confusion attack. Two of the objects in the reference table, t and u, are supposed to be of different types, but actually reference the same object in memory.

```
class U {
    MyObject x;
}
```

Now the applet can run code like this:

```
T t = the pointer tagged T;
U u = the pointer tagged U;
t.x = System.getSecurity(); // the Security Manager
MyObject m = u.x;
```

The result is that the object ends up with a pointer, tagged as having type **MyObject**, to the memory representing Java's Security Manager object. By changing the fields of **m**, the applet can then change the Security Manager, even though the Security Manager's fields have been declared **private**.

While this example showed how type confusion can be used to corrupt the Security Manager, the tactic may be exploited to corrupt virtually any part of the running Java system.

An Example of Type Confusion

Drew Dean discovered a typical type confusion attack, based on Java's handling of array types. Java allows a program that uses a type **T** to use the type *array of* **T**. These array types are not explicitly declared by the programmer but exist automatically. The Java Virtual Machine defines them automatically when they are needed.

These array types are defined by the VM for internal use. Java gives them a name beginning with an open square bracket ([). As this character is not allowed to be the first character of a programmer-defined class name, there is no danger of conflict.

Dean discovered, however, that in Netscape Navigator 3.0β5, a Java byte code file could declare its own type name to be one of the special array type names. Attempting to load such a class would generate an error, but the Java VM would install the name in its internal table anyway.

This redefined one of Java's array types and created a classic type confusion scenario: Java considered the object an array, but it actually had some other type. The result was full system penetration. This problem was fixed in Navigator 3.0β6.

The Type Confusion Tool Kit The Princeton team, as a feasibility demonstration, created a tool kit that allows any type confusion attack to be turned into a disarming of Java's security. In other words, the tool kit serves as a way of turning a small security breach into a complete system penetration. The type confusion tool kit has not been released to the public, and is considered too dangerous to describe in any detail here.

Applets Running Wild

The next security problem is the *Princeton class loader attack*. This was the most widely publicized security breach. The problem was caused by mistakes in the way the Java system integrated separate pieces of code. By corrupting this integration or *linking* process, an attacker could break through Java's security and do anything at all. To better understand this issue, the following section will look more closely at how Java manages the dynamic linking process.

Linking

A Java program is composed of several separate pieces called classes. Each class is stored in a separate file, and the Java system uses a *just in time* strategy to load each class only when it is first needed. Just-in-time fetching allows Java applets to start running quickly, without waiting for the entire applet to be pulled across the Net. It does have one drawback, though: a running applet is usually incomplete. When an applet is built from several code pieces, the system has to be clever enough to make sure that the right pieces are attached in the right places.

A Java class file contains a series of instructions telling the Java system how the class should behave. The instructions sometimes reference other classes by name. Since classes are stored separately, the Java system translates each name into the identity of another class. This may involve loading the mentioned class across the Net.

The core Java system does not do this translation itself, but outsources it to Java objects called Class Loaders. Outsourcing in this way allows programmers to create their own Class Loaders, extending Java's linking mechanism.

The interaction between a Class Loader and the core elements of Java is simple. When Java needs to determine which class corresponds to which name, the following steps are followed:

1. Java calls the Class Loader's **loadClass** method, passing it the name to look up.
2. The Class Loader consults its internal dictionary (which includes a list of built-in classes) to see whether a class with that name already exists. If one exists, that class is returned.
3. If the Class Loader does not have a class with the requested name, it tries to find one. Usually, it does this by fetching the byte code for the class across the Net.
4. After getting the byte code for the class, the Class Loader calls a special method called **defineClass** to turn the byte code into a usable class.
5. When **defineClass** is done, the Class Loader returns the resulting class to Java.

The Class Loader's **loadClass** method returns the class that corresponds to the name being looked up.

There are usually several Class Loaders in operation. When Java needs to translate a name, it asks the Class Loader that originally loaded the class referencing the name. Thus each Class Loader is responsible for maintaining and defining its own part of the *name space*.

Linking and Record-Keeping

Because Java has separate name spaces into which classes can be loaded, it can't simply have a unified "phone directory" tracking which class corresponds to which class name. Instead, the Java Virtual Machine maintains a separate directory for each class. These independent directories keep track of the names needed by each class.

For example, if class **A** has a reference to a class called **B**, the directory for **A** will have an entry for **B** which points to the actual class the name represents. Figure 3.5 shows a more complicated example with four classes referencing each other. A big applet could consist of more than four classes, but the idea is the same: the applet is a set of classes that reference each other.

Attack of the Evil Class Loaders

The example described in Figure 3.5 shows reasonable, self-consistent name spaces. The Princeton team discovered that a hostile Class Loader was capable of setting up a *twisted* name space in which different classes had different views of the Java environment. Such inconsistencies can be exploited to create type confusion. A hostile Class Loader could launch a system penetration attack.

Figure 3.6 shows an example of what an evil Class Loader can do. The figure shows two classes, **A** and **B**, each of which refers to a class name 'C'. However, the two classes have different ideas of what the name 'C' means. Class **A** points to the class we've labeled **C1**, while **B** points to **C2**.

Suppose that the Java code in class **A** allocates an object of type 'C' and then passes that object to class **B**. The Java byte code Verifier thinks

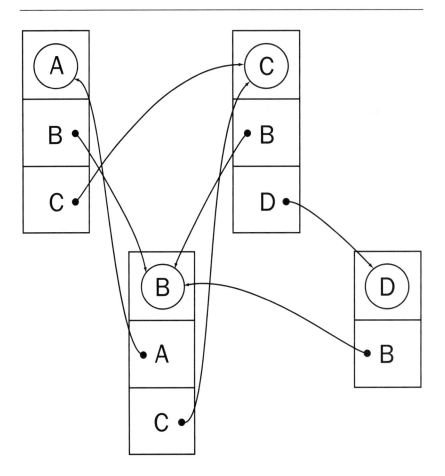

Figure 3.5 Four classes linked together. Each box represents a class. The circled name at the top of each box is the name of the class, and the entries underneath show how the class's name space is defined.

everything is OK, since an object whose class was named '**C**' is being passed into code that is expecting an object whose class name is '**C**'. The

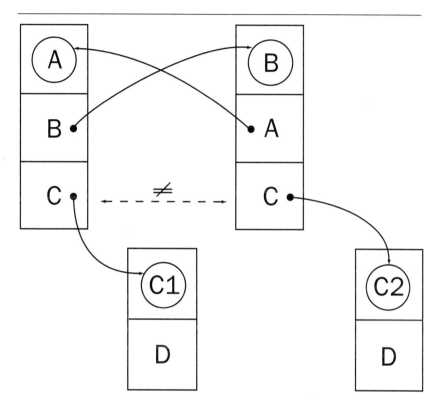

Figure 3.6 An inconsistent name space, created by a hostile Class Loader. Classes **A** and **B** have different ideas about what **C** refers to. This can sometimes be used to confuse the Class Loader.

Verifier allows the operation to proceed. But when class **B** accesses the object named '**C**', the true type will be **C1**, not the **C2** that the Verifier approved. An object of type **C1** is being treated as though it were of class **C2**. This is type confusion.

When this attack is carried out, the evil Class Loader is asked twice to say which class corresponds to the name '**C**'. It gives back different answers: **C1** for class **A**, and **C2** for class **B**.

Taking Exception

The Class Loader attack should have been impossible. Java's security rules prohibit applets from creating Class Loaders. Unfortunately, the Princeton team discovered a flaw in the byte code Verifier that allowed this rule to be violated. Nothing stops an applet from declaring a new class that is a subclass of the **ClassLoader** superclass. It is up to the Security Manager to stop the actual construction from occurring. In this case, the Security Manager check is bypassed because of a bug. Read on for the gory details.

The rule against making Class Loaders is enforced by the object-oriented nature of Java. Every Java class extends its superclass. Each class can be thought of as being a specialized version of its superclass.* Every class has one or more constructor functions, which properly initialize new objects. Java requires each constructor to call the constructor of its superclass before it does anything else. For example, if you create a class called **MyHashtable** which extends the built-in class **java.util.Hashtable**, then you have to provide a constructor for **MyHashtable**. That constructor must call the constructor of **java.util.Hashtable** before it does anything else. The byte code Verifier ensures that these rules are followed.

To prevent applets from making Class Loaders, the constructor for the class **ClassLoader** consults the Security Manager, which generates a Security Exception if the Class Loader being constructed would belong to an applet. This Security Exception can abort the creation of such an object. If an applet defines a new **EvilClassLoader** class to extend the basic ClassLoader, then the new constructor is required to call Java's basic ClassLoader constructor. Doing so generates a Security Exception which prevents the applet from creating an **EvilClassLoader**.

What the Princeton team discovered was a trick by which a constructor could avoid calling its superclass constructor, without being

---

* One particular class, **java.lang.Object**, has no superclass.

caught by the Verifier. This allowed them to create an **EvilClassLoader** whose constructor did not call the basic ClassLoader constructor, and thus was not subject to the normal Security Manager check. The **EvilClassLoader** could then create type confusion.

Having created type confusion, the attacker could then exploit it to achieve full system intrusion. That is, the attacker could do anything at all on the victim's machine.

The (Sort of) Fix

Sun Microsystems and Netscape had two options for fixing this problem. They could prevent the superclass-constructor-avoidance by fixing the Verifier, or they could find another way of forcing the basic Class Loader constructor to be called. They chose to do the latter. They added an **initialized** data field to every Class Loader, and set the field to **true** only when the basic Class Loader constructor was run. Class Loader would refuse to perform the crucial **defineClass** action unless the **initialized** field was **true**.

The implementation created a new private Class Loader method called **defineClass0**. This does the real work of **defineClass**. Redefining **defineClass** to check the **initialized** flag and call **defineClass0** only if the flag was **true** helps to block this particular security hole. The change does not prevent an attacker from making a Class Loader, but it does prevent an attacker from using the new Class Loader once it has been made.

The change took effect in Netscape Navigator 2.02. Unfortunately, future attacks managed to circumvent this fix.

The Reaction

This flaw received more press coverage than any of the others. It had more news interest than the DNS bug because it was more serious. Later bugs did not receive as much coverage because by the time they came to light, the novelty had worn off. That does not mean that the current and future security problems are not just as serious. Whether or not security problems are splashed on the front pages, they still need to be taken seriously.

Perhaps the press coverage partly reflected a backlash against the extremely positive hype surrounding most press stories about Java at the time. Java is great, but many of the exaggerated claims went much too far. There was even a story stating that if you wrote programs in Java you would never have to debug them because they would always be right the first time. To be fair, only a little of the hype came from Sun. Much of it came from freelance consultants, self-proclaimed experts, and trainers who had an interest in seeing *their* Java bandwagon become a juggernaut.

When the applets-running-wild flaw was discovered, Sun Microsystems, Netscape, and the flaw's discoverers gained some valuable experience discussing these issues with each other, and with the press. As a result the parties did a better job of conveying simple and consistent information to the public. Hopefully, this will remain true when future security holes come to light.

Casting Caution to the Wind

Software consultant Tom Cargill has discovered two security flaws related to the way Java handles interface types. Both flaws involve a rare case in which Java fails to check whether a method is private. Both also use type casting operations on Java's interface types. By exploiting these flaws, an attacker can call private methods normally prohibited by Java's security rules. Since some of the security-critical values inside the Java system are protected by private methods, a complete security breach using this attack is possible.

Simple Interface Casting

The core of Cargill's first discovery is shown in the following code:

```
interface Inter {
    void f();


}
class Secure implements Inter {
```

```
    private void f();
}


class Dummy extends Secure implements Inter {
    public void f();


    Dummy() {
        Secure s = new Secure();
        Inter i = (Inter) s;
        i.f();              // should be illegal
    }
}
```

This code allows the private **f** method of class **Secure** to be called illegally. The Java interpreter fails to determine if **f** is private when **i.f()** is called.

The Princeton team figured out how to use this flaw to achieve full system penetration. This was done by exploiting the fix to the Class Loader bug. The Class Loader bug was fixed by splitting the critical **defineClass** method into a private method and a public method. The private method, **defineClass0**, did the work. The public method checked the **initialized** flag and called **defineClass0** only if the flag was **true**. Since the private **defineClass0** method couldn't be called directly by an applet, this was supposed to fix the Class Loader bug.

Unfortunately, a variant of the interface casting trick shown here allows an applet to call the private **defineClass0** method directly, bypassing the check. This meant that the attack could create a Class Loader by exploiting the Verifier bug. The initialized flag would be false, but that wouldn't matter. A programmer could bypass the flag-check by exploiting the interface casting trick to call the private **defineClass0** method directly.

By using this trick, an attacker could gain full system penetration under Netscape Navigator 2.02.

The Full Fix

Netscape fixed this problem in two ways. First, they fixed the flaw in their Java Virtual Machine that allowed the interface casting trick to work. Second, they began storing and checking the initialized flag inside the Java Virtual Machine, rather than in programmer-generated Java code. Netscape eliminated the dangerous **defineClass0** operation by integrating everything into the VM's implementation of **defineClass.** This change took effect in Navigator 3.0β3.

In reaction to the interface casting bug, Netscape changed their Java implementation to protect itself more generally against an attacker who had the ability to call private methods. By going beyond a simple bug-fix to improve the structure of the system, Netscape practiced good security engineering. Their decision paid off when the next bug was discovered.

Advanced Interface Casting

Here is the core of Cargill's second discovery:

```
interface Inter {

    void f();

}



class Secure implements Inter {
    private void f();
}
```

```
class Dummy implements Inter {
   public void f();



   static void attack() {
       Inter inter[2] = {new Dummy(), new Secure() };
       for(int j=0; j<2; ++j)        inter[j].f();

   }

}
```

The first call, **inter[0].f()** is legal since **Dummy**'s **f** method is public. The next time around the loop, **inter[1].f()** is illegal since **Secure**'s **f** method is private.

In this case, Java was too smart for its own good. In order to improve performance, it only checked for legality the first time through the loop. Theoretically, what was legal the first time would be legal the next time. (See Chapter 2.) Though this is often a correct assumption, it broke down for the code shown above.

This trick allows an attacker to call private methods in violation of Java's security rules. Had Netscape not improved the structure of their system after the previous bug was reported, this bug would have once again allowed the Class Loader attack to work. However, because Netscape had protected their system against private method attacks, this flaw was not easy to exploit.

Tag-Team Applets

The next group of attacks combines the two previous attack methods. By setting up two separate naming environments and passing objects between them, this new group of attacks causes type confusion, leading to security breaches.

These attacks are launched by putting two applets on a Web page, and having the two applets cooperate. Typically, both applets would be written by the same programmer, and located on the same Web server.

To better understand this threat, the next section will examine in further detail how Java manages name spaces. (See also Chapter 2.)

What's in a Name?

In a Java-enabled browser, several applets might be running at the same time. Since each applet contains several classes, each with a distinct name, there's a danger that two applets might accidentally use the same name. To prevent this, the Java designers decreed there should be a separate name space for each applet. That is, each applet should have its own view of which names correspond to which classes.

Despite the fact that each applet has its own name space, there are ways for two applets to pass objects back and forth among themselves. One such channel involves **public** variables in the Java runtime. Another channel is through manipulating threads. The result is that an applet can potentially have an object whose name is defined in another name space.

Things can get tricky when this happens. For example, suppose that the **AncientGreek** applet and the **Simpsons** applet are running at the same time. Each of the two applets has defined a class called **Homer**, but they have very different ideas of how **Homer** should behave. Worse yet, imagine that the two applets communicate, and the **AncientGreek** applet ends up with a **Homer Simpson** object. If the **AncientGreek** applet asks the object what its class is, the object responds, **Homer**. The **AncientGreek** applet then asks **Homer** to recite an epic poem. Depending on your point of view, the result would be either tragic or comical. In any case, it wouldn't be what the programmers wanted.

This isn't really a security risk. However, it becomes one if the Java system itself gets confused. The danger is that the system will decide that two unlike types are really the same, when all that is the same is their names. This sort of mix-up would constitute type confusion, and the applet could break the Java type system, leading to a security breach.

One way that an applet could do this is by engaging in *type punning*. The applet would set up two types with the same name, create an object of one type, and then use it as though it were an object of the other type. For example, suppose that this is a Java type:

```
class Secure {
    private Object secretData;
}
```

Another applet could create another type with the same name:

```
class Secure {      // impostor
    public Object secretData;
}
```

Now if the applet could get an object of the real **Secure** class, and convince Java that the object belonged to the impostor **Secure** class, Java would allow the applet to access the supposedly private **secretData** field. As far as Java is concerned, this would be fine. The impostor **secretData** field is public. The applet would have accessed data it was not supposed to see.

Type punning works for method calls, too. If the **secretData** field were replaced with a **dangerousOperation** method, then an applet that could do type punning could call the **dangerousOperation** method even though it was supposed to be private. In summary, if type punning is possible, Java's security collapses.

Java prevents type punning by being very careful when deciding whether two classes are the same. Rather than using the class name to make this decision, Java considers two classes the same only if they have the same name and were defined in the same name space (that is, by the same Class Loader). That is sufficient protection to avoid type punning.

What Went Wrong: A Name Alone

Unfortunately, the creators of Java were not always so careful. In Java 1.0.2, Netscape 2.02, and the first beta version of Internet Explorer, the types of interfaces and exceptions were compared by name rather than by (name, name space) pair as required. This led to a set of attacks that could break Java's security system, achieving full system penetration.

The attacks worked as described above. The attacker wrote two applets defining different classes with the same name **C**. One applet would create an object of class **C** and pass it to the other applet, which would operate on its **C**. This leads to a classic type confusion situation, which can be exploited by methods seen several times in this chapter.

Big Attacks Come in Small Packages

Our final attack applet exploits a Java security weakness in beta versions of Microsoft's Internet Explorer 3.0. The weakness allows code in an untrusted applet to pass itself off as part of a Java package. This flaw allows an attacker to gain full access to the victim's files and to the network.

Understanding this flaw requires a more detailed explanation of Java packages.

Java Packages

The Java language supports the concept of packages—groups of Java classes meant to be used together. Packages have names like **java.lang** and **EDU.princeton.cs.sip**. Every Java class belongs to some package.

Packages serve two purposes. First, since the full name of a class is the package name followed by the class name, they provide a way for different people to name their classes without having accidental name collisions. For example, if we put all of our classes into the authors package and you put all of your classes into the readers package, then our class names cannot collide with yours.

The second purpose of packages is to restrict access to certain Java variables. When declaring a variable, a programmer states which classes are allowed to access the variable. If the variable is declared **private**, it is accessible only by the class which created it. If a variable is declared **protected**, it is accessible only by the creating class and its subclasses. If a variable is declared **public**, it is accessible by all classes. If a variable is declared neither private, protected, nor public, then it is accessible only by classes in the creating class's package.

Some packages limit their membership to only built-in browser classes. Membership is restricted by having the Virtual Machine ask the Security Manager to pass judgment on every request to join a package. The Security Manager enforces restrictions by prohibiting classes loaded across the Net from joining restricted packages. (For more information on this topic, see Chapter 5.)

What Went Wrong

In Microsoft's browser, there was an error in the way the Security Manager made its decisions about package membership. Because of the bug, the Security Manager incorrectly used only the first component of the package name to check access permission. This method failed for packages whose names started with **com.ms**. Interestingly, several of Microsoft's built-in packages started this way.

The result was that untrusted applet code could join a sensitive package, and gain access to any variables in that class that were accessible package-wide. These variables included, among other things, the Security Manager's list of files to which the applet had access. A mischievous applet could access any file on the system by changing the Security Manager's list to include the desired file.

The Reaction

This flaw was found just before Microsoft was to ship the first non-beta version of their Internet Explorer 3.0 browser. Since the ship date had been announced (and a big public release hoopla was planned), the ship date could not be moved. Since the product had a serious security flaw, shipping it was not an acceptable alternative. Microsoft's development team launched an heroic effort to fix the bug, test the solution, and restart the product release cycle in time to meet the original release deadline. They succeeded.

What These Problems Teach Us

The designers of Java tried to ensure that applets could not misbehave. Though they claim success, (with apologies to Mr. Clemens) claims about Java's security have been greatly exaggerated.

Recent implementations of Java have had some rather serious security flaws. Several attacks have been detailed in this chapter. Two of the attacks led the CERT Coordination Center to direct that the Java capabilities of some Web browsers be disabled [CERT, 1996a; CERT, 1996b]. Turning Java off is certainly one solution, but not a very satisfying one. Users of Java-enabled browsers who want to surf the Web safely should probably enable Java only when they know they are going to a safe Web site. Either that, or browse the Web on a machine that has neither private data nor mission-critical importance.

Each of the security problems that we discussed in this chapter can be implemented as an attack applet. In fact, the Princeton team regularly creates attack applets in the lab (on a protected network, of course) to test the limits of Java's vulnerabilities.* Though rumor has it that attack applets based on the DNS bug and the Princeton Class Loader attack have appeared on underground Web sites, there is no convincing evidence that such attack applets have ever been used to crack a system on the Net. Nonetheless, the main reason attack applets need to be taken very seriously is that the end result of a successful attack is full system penetration. In other words, attack applets are capable of aiding a hacker in taking over your machine.

Java brings the formidable power of executable content to the Web. Trading security for this power is a tough pill to swallow, but a pill that's probably worth ingesting. Users want audio-visual conferencing without cross-network eavesdropping. Users want loosely coupled computation for things like factoring without cycle theft and denial of service. Users want games without Trojan horses. Users want **save** and **restore** for applet-based preferences without having their valuable files stolen. Being security conscious, users can probably have what they want, without getting anything that they don't need.

---

* The machines the Princeton team attacks are always machines in their lab.

Chapter 4

Malicious Applets
A common nuisance

The previous chapter discussed the most serious security flaws found in Java to date. All of the flaws described have been fixed. An attack applet is any applet implementing any of the attacks described in the last chapter. Fortunately there have been no confirmed sightings of attack applets outside the lab. But there is another more pervasive kind of hostile applet, not as serious a security concern, but still worthy of attention: the malicious applet.

Unlike their attack applet cousins, malicious applets *have* escaped the lab. Such realities make it necessary for all users of Java-enabled browsers to be aware of Java security threats. Simply surfing over to a Web page containing a hostile applet allows it to invade your machine with its malicious code. This chapter explores many malicious applets, ranging from the merely annoying to the more seriously disturbing.

Near the beginning of Chapter 2, classes of potential Java threats were discussed. The four classes of attacks named were: system modification attacks, invasion of privacy attacks, denial of service attacks, and antagonistic attacks. Java is a powerful enough language that, without security constraints placed on applets, it is possible to implement all four such classes of attacks. The Java security model was designed to thwart those threats perceived to be the greatest dangers.

The previous chapter taught us that the original Java security model had some serious flaws. The most serious problems result in intrusions that allow arbitrary system modification (effectively, unlimited access). An attack applet based on one of these strategies constitutes a cracker breaking into your machine.

It is true that the attacks of the previous chapter require an in-depth understanding of both Java and the Internet. It has been argued that we should feel fairly confident that few people will be able to exploit such esoteric vulnerabilities. That is a dangerous position to take. One instance of a cracker discovering a novel attack applet will change such statements considerably. Once loose, attack applet information would quickly spread throughout the cracker community. Our job as security researchers is to find security holes and plug them *before* they are used by dishonest people. Security researchers also work to create such a secure model that holes are very rare. Fortunately, none of the serious attacks have shown up in the form of attack applets, though the possibility looms ominously.

Don't breathe a sigh of relief yet. Tampering with Java security does not always require wizardry. In fact, writing Java code to breach security can be easy. This chapter discusses some simple Java applets gone bad. Such applets are known on the Net as *malicious applets*. Entire collections are available for anyone interested to see, to adapt, and to use [LaDue, 1996; DigiCrime, 1996; Graffiti, 1996]. The best first defense against these sorts of applets is to learn about them.

What Is a Malicious Applet?

A malicious applet is any applet that attacks the local system of a Web surfer using one of the three less serious classes of attacks discussed in Chapter 2. Malicious applets involve denial of service, invasion of privacy, and/or annoyance. Malicious applets are written by crackers and other Net miscreants to harass, annoy, and damage Java users. They can even seriously damage a Java user's machine. Any applet that performs an action against the will of the user who invoked it should be considered malicious.

It is important to emphasize again that use of the term Java user applies equally to Java developers *and* people surfing the Web with a Java-enabled browser. Using Java does not require any programming, or even possession of the JDK. It is enough to use a Java-enabled browser. Under this definition, most people who surf the Web (85% of whom use Java-savvy Netscape) are Java users.

Malicious applets exist on the Web today that do the following bad things:

- forge mail from you to whomever the evil applet's author chooses saying whatever they wish while *masquerading as you*
- steal your CPU cycles to perform their own work while your legitimate processes languish
- crash your local system by using all available system resources.

This is an impressive and daunting list of activities, and it only scratches the surface.

There are also malicious applets created simply to annoy. These applets go only a bit too far, lingering at the edge of respectability. These sorts of applets do things like play sound files continuously, set up threads that monitor your Web use, and display unwanted graphics on your screen.

Stopping Malicious Applets Before They Start

What can be done to stop malicious applets from doing their evil deeds? At the moment, nothing. The safest thing to do is to avoid unknown and untrusted Web sites unless you first disable Java. Just by using a Java-enabled browser to surf the Web, you are open to attack by both attack applets and malicious applets. This danger, combined with the serious attacks discussed in Chapter 3, has caused the CERT Coordination Center to recommend disabling Java when surfing untrusted sites [CERT, 1996a; CERT, 1996b].

What can be done to stop these applets from doing their evil deeds in the future? There are many possibilities. One especially interesting approach would be to write detectors for bad applets based on known vulnerabilities. That way they could be screened out by the byte code Verifier (or some similar extension). Princeton's Safe Internet Programming group is performing research in this detection area now.

Another way to protect against malicious applets is by improving Java's security model. Additions are currently in the works and may be made available as this book is released. The security model can be improved by placing limitations on resources that applets can use. An additional improvement promised for delivery soon is the ability to use a kind of encryption called digital signing to authenticate the origin of an applet. Using this technology, a Web surfer could specify a list of *trusted* sites whose applets should be allowed to run without restrictions. These solutions along with a host of others are discussed in Chapter 5. It is very likely that some of the planned improvements to Java security will safely allow more liberal (and transparent) Java use.

The next few sections will discuss various kinds of malicious applets. Starting with the least worrisome category, the merely annoying, the text will progress through the truly malicious machine-hangers. Possible motives for creating these applets will be discussed along the way. Keep in mind while you read this chapter, that the malicious applets described here pale in comparison with the attack applets described in Chapter 3. Fortunately, the security researchers who discovered those vulnerabilities are the good guys.

Disabling Java

There are certainly many unsavory characters on the Net, and many of them have created similarly unsavory Web pages. If for some reason you wish to check such sites out, it would be a good idea to disable Java first.

The best way to protect yourself from malicious applets is to disable Java when surfing dangerous Web sites. Much like being streetwise in a big city, your choice to use or disable Java will depend on what browsing you will be doing. If you keep to the sites of big business, you are less likely to find dangerous applets, just as the finance districts of New York and Chicago are less dangerous than the housing projects. Know where you are on the Web, and take precautions accordingly.

Disabling Java in Netscape Navigator 2.0x Disabling Java under Netscape Navigator 2.0x is easy and can be done in the midst of a session. Re-enabling Java is also possible, should you change your mind. Figure 4.1 explains how Java can be disabled in Netscape Navigator 2.0x.

Disabling Java in Netscape Navigator 3.x It is also possible to disable Java in the newest version of Netscape, but the mechanism differs from previous versions. It is harder to find, but Figure 4.2 illustrates the process.

Disabling Java in Internet Explorer 3.x Internet Explorer also allows Java to be disabled. Figure 4.3 explains how Java can be disabled in Internet Explorer 3.x.

Figure 4.1 Disabling Java in Netscape Navigator 2.0x. Open the *Options* menu and select the *Security Preferences* option. Doing this will open a dialog window like the one shown here. The button for disabling Java is at the top of the window. Java is disabled when the button is pressed *in*. Java is enabled by default.

Annoying Applets

The simplest kind of malicious applet is only annoying. Malicious applets of this type do things just beyond acceptable. Because Java has exceptionally powerful multimedia packages, annoying applets can do a large variety of things, ranging from playing sound files continuously, to displaying obscene pictures.

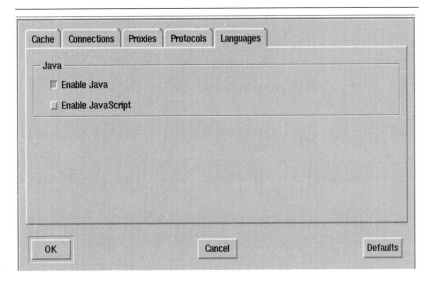

Figure 4.2 Disabling Java in Netscape Navigator 3.x. Open the *Options* menu and select the *Network Preferences* option. This will open a tabbed dialog window. Select the Languages tab. You will see a dialog window like the one shown here. The button to enable/disable Java is apparent. Java is enabled when the button is pressed *in*.

One particularly humorous annoying applet opens a dialog box with the message *April Fools* and an **OK** button. Users naturally think the applet is supposed to exit when you click **OK** as it says on the screen. But the dialog box zips around the screen, avoiding the mouse as the user tries to click **OK**. This quirk renders the applet difficult to stop through normal means. The easiest way to get rid of it is to exit the browser.

Listing 4.1 provides the code for another annoying applet based on an idea from Mark LaDue.* This applet appears to be well-behaved,

---

* Mark LaDue is a Mathematics grad student at Georgia Tech who put together the Hostile Applet Home Page [LaDue, 1996].

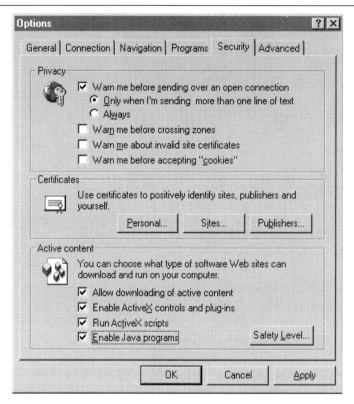

Figure 4.3 Disabling Java in Microsoft Internet Explorer 3.x. Open the *View* menu and select *Options.* This will open a tabbed dialog window. Select the *Security* tab. Once that tab is chosen, a dialog window like the one shown here will appear. The checkbox for enable/disable Java is at the bottom of the window. Java is enabled when the box is checked.

at first. All it does is display a nice little picture of one of the author's dogs (and baby Jack). It also plays some appropriate background sound (the dog barking). Not all that exciting for an applet. The code is shown in Listing 4.1.

Listing 4.1 NoisyApplet sustains a thread past the time its creating class is unloaded.

```
/*  NoisyApplet.java                                    */
/*  Adapted from the NoisyBear applet of Mark LaDue.   */
/*  You will need a sound file and a picture to make   */
/*  this work.                                          */
/*  This applet is provided solely as an example and   */
/*  is not guaranteed to do anything.                   */
/*  Use it at your own risk.                            */


import java.applet.AudioClip;
import java.awt.*;


public class NoisyApplet extends java.applet.Applet
implements Runnable {
    Font msgFont = new Font("TimesRoman", Font.PLAIN, 36);
    Thread noisethread = null;   // thread to run sound in
    Image jackImage;
    Image offscreenImage;
    Graphics offscreenGraphics;
    AudioClip bark;              // sound file variable


    // the init() runs to set things up
    public void init() {
        // first, set up the picture
        jackImage getImage(getCodeBase(), "jack+waldog.jpg");
```

```
        offscreenImage = createImage(this.size().width,
                        this.size().height);
        offscreenGraphics = offscreenImage.getGraphics();
        // then load the audio file
        bark = getAudioClip(getCodeBase(), "bark.au");
    }


// the start() method runs whenever you enter the
// applet's page. it also runs after init()
public void start()  {
    // start a thread to run the audio clip in
    if (noisethread == null)  {
        noisethread = new Thread(this);
        noisethread.start();
    }
}


// the stop() method runs when you exit
// the applet's page
public void stop() {
    if (noisethread != null) {
        // uncommenting the following 2 lines will stop
        // the sound
        // if (bark != null)
        //     bark.stop();
        noisethread.stop();
```

```
        noisethread = null;
    }
}


//  this starts the ball rolling by telling the sound
//  to "go"
public void run() {
    if (bark != null) bark.loop();
}


// the paint() method draws the graphics
public void paint(Graphics g) {
    int jack_width = jackImage.getWidth(this);
    int jack_height = jackImage.getHeight(this);

    offscreenGraphics.drawImage(jackImage, 0, 0,
      jack_width, jack_height, this);
    offscreenGraphics.setColor(Color.white);
    offscreenGraphics.setColor(Color.red);
    offscreenGraphics.setFont(msgFont);
    offscreenGraphics.drawString(
      "Walnut says HI HI HI ...", 150, 225);
    // actually draw the image
    g.drawImage(offscreenImage, 0, 0, this);
}
}
```

This applet has been tested and proven to be annoying on a large number of platform/browser combinations including: Netscape 2.0x/SunOs 4.1.3, Netscape 2.0x and 3.0*β* /Windows 95, Netscape 2.0x/SGI-IRIX, Netscape 2.0x/Solaris, Netscape 3.0*β*/Linux, and Internet Explorer 3.0*β*2/Windows 95. The code was compiled with JDK 1.0.2 for testing.

What makes the **NoisyApplet** annoying is that the sound never stops, even if the user surfs to another Web page. How could this happen? Simple; the applet starts a thread that never stops!

Why does the sound keep on going? As you can see in the Listing 4.2, the **stop()** method of the NoisyApplet class has been redefined. The redefinition makes the thread live until the user either figures out how to kill the thread, disable audio on their machine, or quit the browser.[*] None of these options are particularly convenient.

Listing 4.2 Spinning a thread forever.

```
public void stop() {
    if (noisethread != null)  {
        // uncommenting the following 2 lines will
        // stop the sound
        // if (bark != null)
        //     bark.stop();
        noisethread.stop();
        noisethread = null;
    }
}
```

---

[*]   Disabling Java after this applet starts barking does nothing to kill the runaway thread.

The lines commented out would silence our NoisyApplet by installing a more normal **stop()** method. By commenting out these lines you can turn our somewhat-typical applet into a malicious annoyance. Clearly, the line between an honest mistake and an antagonistic programming practice is very fine indeed.

There are some interesting implications that our simple annoying applet introduces. Any thread can employ the same strategy of redefining the **stop()** method in order to run *ad infinitum*. Depending on the way a Security Manager is written, Java may not require a programmer to stop all threads. Overriding the default **stop()** method is, as we have shown, a trivial exercise. Threads can run even in the absence of the applet that spawned them. This means that it is possible to write threads that monitor what the user is doing.

The Business Assassin Applet

One such monitoring applet (possibly an armchair exercise) is called the Business Assassin applet [Dean et al., 1996; OBC, 1996]. The Business Assassin targets the applets of a particular Web site, such as applets from Gamelan (**http://www.gamelan.com**).

If you place this applet on your home page, it will start up threads on the remote machine of anyone who surfs your site with Java enabled. These threads silently watch for other applets being loaded from Gamelan. If the monitoring threads detect the user surfing the Gamelan Web site, they begin the attack. The malicious threads make useless any applets coming in from Gamelan. They kill the threads of Gamelan applets (something discussed in more detail on page 118). Another feature of the Business Assassin applet (code disabled by default) goes on to launch a denial of service attack against anyone who visits Gamelan after running the Assassin.

On the surface, the Business Assassin applet appears to be harmless. That is because it uses threads to do all the dirty work. Threads are not required to stop running when an applet's Web page is exited. This means that threads can keep running in the browser after an applet has appeared to finish. In order to have the blame pinned on some other applet, hostile threads can be programmed to delay their attack until some future time. In the case of the Assassin's threads, an apparent bug in the Security Manager allows the Assassin threads to attack thread groups that do not belong to it. It waits for the target threads from Gamelan to appear and only then initiates hostile activity.

Applets like the Business Assassin will certainly have a chilling effect on Web-based commerce. Even if applets that use never-ending threads are not used for annoying things like these, they still have the potential to be used for information gathering. If an applet can spawn a monitoring thread, there is no reason that it could not report information it finds interesting back to its server. Such information could include lists of sites a user has visited, files that he or she has downloaded, the names of other competing applets run, or a host of other things. Such monitoring applets should be named *BigBrother*.

Denial of Service

In a cracker's world, the next best thing to breaking in to your computer is locking you out of it. After all, if the cracker cannot use your computer, then neither should you! Attacks that prevent someone from using their machine are called denial of service attacks in the security community. Denial of service comes in many guises. Attacks may involve consuming all available CPU cycles, allocating every last bit of memory, or hogging all possible screen space. The one common requirement is that the user being attacked is effectively locked out of their machine. An effective denial of service attack happens so quickly that it's usually impossible to stop it. Experiencing such an attack is a sobering event.

There are many ways to write applets initiating denial of service attacks. We think these attacks are serious enough that code for them will not be listed here. Examining some attacks through high-level description, and occasional code fragments, should be enough to illustrate a point. Realistically, the sorts of malicious applets being described are not too difficult to dream up. People who are interested will be able to either create the code or find it, as they see fit.

Consider the denial of service attack presented in Listing 4.3. It recycles an idea from the **NoisyApplet** making use of non-terminating threads. Quite simple to formulate, it looks something like this:

1. Create an applet that starts a thread with its priority set to **MAX_PRIORITY**. This makes the thread run as quickly as possible and gives it a leg up in the ongoing competition between processes for CPU time.
2. Redefine **stop()** to null for the thread.
3. Do something silly in the main part of the applet so that it appears to be harmless. Show a picture or display some cute animation.
4. Have the thread **sleep** for a while to delay its malicious activities. This will have the effect of placing the blame somewhere else when the thread wakes back up to perform its dirty work.
5. When the thread wakes up, have it begin calculating in an infinite loop (or some other CPU intensive activity that eats cycles). This will, in effect, bring the browser down by taking away all available computational resources. One particularly worthy function for intense calculation overload is the Ackerman function shown in Listing 4.3.

Listing 4.3 The Ackerman function implemented as a Java application. Ackerman takes integer *n* and exponentiates *n* by itself *n* times. This means that Ackerman(3) is equivalent to three cubed, cubed. The program can be run by typing the command "java Ackerman *n*", where *n* is an integer. Computing anything greater than Ackerman(3) takes a long time and many CPU cycles. This code was written to be as inefficient as possible. This version of Ackerman could easily be used in a denial of service attack.

```java
import java.lang.System;

import java.io.IOException;

import java.lang.Math;


class Ackerman {
public static void main(String[] args) {
    long ackValue = 1;
    long exp = 0;

    if (args.length >= 1) {
        try  { exp = Integer.parseInt(args[0]); }
        catch (NumberFormatException e)  { exp = 0; }
    }

    if (exp > 1) {
        ackValue = exp;
        int numLoops = (int)exp;
        for (int i = 1; i < numLoops; i++) {
            exp = ackValue;
```

```
        for (int j = 1; j < numLoops; j++) {
            ackValue = ackValue * exp;
            System.out.println("current value is "
                            + ackValue);
        }
    }
}
System.out.println("Ackerman value: " + ackValue);
}
}
```

This denial of service approach is simple and elegant. There are literally hundreds of things that can be done as the step five. Other possibilities include endlessly appending to a **StringBuffer** and using **drawString** to display its entire contents. This ends up as a double whammy eating both CPU cycles *and* memory. Another possibility would be calculating π using the most inefficient algorithm possible. If you have trouble remembering how to code poorly, just teach an introductory programming course to jog your memory.

On a more serious note, this line of attack is both very simple and very successful. Most browsers will seize up and die under such an attack.

Applets that implement these strategies exist on the Web now. Skeptical readers are welcome to surf over and kill their browser personally (**http://www.math.gatech.edu/~mladue/HostileApplets .html**). Just surf to a Web page containing hostile applets using a Java-enabled browser and they will automatically be invoked. Nothing can be done to prevent them. Chapter 5 examines some strategies for protection, but they are all still in early development. Just to complicate matters, such a hostile applet can implicate other Web pages by using delay tactics discussed previously.

Is Denial of Service All That Bad?

There is no doubt that denial of service attacks are less serious than security breaches of the sort we discussed in Chapter 3. Although a browser might be crashed with such attacks, intruders will not gain entry into a system. This has led some people at Javasoft to dismiss this class of attacks as unimportant. Before Arthur van Hoff (one of the original designers of Java) left Javasoft for a private venture, he posted a note to **comp.lang.java** that dismissed such problems as either not very serious or a concern for browser vendors—not Javasoft. Although the most serious security problems should be addressed first, denial of service applets should also be addressed. Using resource allocation limitations (Chapter 5) is one line of defense. Threads should not be able to override the **stop()** method so easily, either.

It is ironic that some of the most Java-heavy Web pages almost go as far as denial of service in doing what their programmers intended. Some Java-enhanced sites take quite a while to load (we have heard of some applets that take ten minutes to start up even over a very fast T1 connection). The bottleneck likely involves the byte code Verification process and not the network transmission time. Of course, slow loading/verifying really doesn't constitute a true denial of service attack.

Opening Untrusted Windows

A more serious denial of service attack than browser-killers involves opening large numbers of very large windows. There are a couple of reasons why this kind of attack should be considered more severe. The side-effects of this attack tend to freeze access to the keyboard and mouse while the applet runs. This makes the applet harder to control. Also, the way these windows are created and mapped makes it possible to pop up untrusted Java applet windows without the mandatory warning they are supposedly required to display.

A denial of service applet based on this idea would be very similar to the ones we discussed on page 107, with the addition of the window-popping code shown here:

```
// In the code below, littleWindow is of type Frame
// Adapted from an idea by Mark LaDue
try {
// create a window
littleWindow = new bigFrame("Whocares");
// make it very big
littleWindow.resize(1000000, 1000000);
// position it to cover everything
littleWindow.move(-1000, -1000);
// finally, open the window
littleWindow.show();
}
catch (OutOfMemoryError o) {}
repaint();
}
class bigFrame extends Frame {          // constructor method
    Label 1;
    bigFrame(String title)     {
        super(title);
        setLayout(new GridLayout(1, 1));
        Canvas whiteCanvas = new Canvas();
        whiteCanvas.setBackground(Color.white);
        add(whiteCanvas);
```

```
        }
}
```

This code will open a very large (one-million by one-million pixel) white window without the supposedly mandatory untrusted Java applet window message. Put this code in a loop so many windows pile on top of each other, and *violá*, an applet that consumes major resources in an interesting new way.

The act of generating many windows all at the same time causes many window events to fill the window manager's event queue. This effectively disables the mouse and keyboard, since they talk to the machine through window events themselves. The console of the workstation displaying these very large windows freezes up. There are two things a user may do when an attack like this is leveled against them: go to another machine on the same network and kill the offending browser processes, or reboot.

The ability to open a window without the mandatory untrusted window banner is interesting in its own right. Using variants of such code, it is possible to spoof Web site password panels. This leads to interesting social engineering attacks wherein an unsuspecting user is asked to provide their password due to a spurious security alert event. Many users fall for such schemes. After collecting login and password information, a malicious applet can mail off the information to a collection site for later use by a cracker.

Stealing Cycles

Theoretical computer science teaches that some computational problems are much harder than others. Very hard problems scale exponentially. Other problems are solvable in Polynomial time, but only using an *oracle* that can correctly decide which path to follow each time a choice is encountered. Each member of the second set of problems is termed *NP-Hard*. According to Murphey's Computational Law, any interesting problem will be computationally infeasible.

One of the most perplexing problems in computer science was introduced in 1977 by three cryptography researchers named Rivest, Shamir, and Adelman. They invented a sophisticated encryption algorithm which they called RSA, after their initials. The only known Achille's heel of the RSA cryptosystem rests on the ability (or inability, rather) to factor a very large integer into a product of prime numbers in a reasonable length of time. The exact complexity of prime factoring is not known, but it is expected to be difficult, and has proven to be so thus far.

One particular instance of the RSA problem involves factoring a specific 129-digit number into its prime components. Using theoretical computer science as a guide, Rivest, Shamir, and Adelman estimated that it would take 4×10^{16} years to factor RSA-129. However, applying the quadratic sieve algorithm along with the collaboration of thousands of volunteers (who donated CPU time on their workstations), researchers solved RSA-129 in 1994 after less than a year of work. The key to the solution was using thousands of computers at the same time to attack the factoring problem. To prove that they had discovered the proper solution, the distributed-factoring researchers used their solution to break a secret coded message that Rivest, Shamir, and Adelman had created in 1977 as a test. The message read: "The magic words are squeamish ossifrage."

Java offers a unique opportunity for use in cooperative projects such as factoring RSA-129. Some of the researchers involved in factoring RSA-129 recently announced they had also factored RSA-130—in a fraction of the time. Java would make cooperative efforts much easier through platform independence.

So what does this have to do with malicious applets? One critical feature of the RSA efforts was the voluntary participation. That is what made them *cooperative* efforts. The same sort of factoring could be accomplished using a malicious applet. Such an applet would surreptitiously steal CPU cycles from the machine of any Web user who hit its Web page. The applet would spin a thread on the remote machine to run part of a factoring solution on that machine's CPU. After a sufficient amount of work, a partial solution could be mailed back to a collection site for collation with similar results from elsewhere.

There is no reason a CPU cycle stealing applet needs to work on factoring. It can perform any work. Using such an applet, a Web miscreant could instantly upgrade their 486-DX2/66 into a huge collective machine with the combined power of hundreds of workstations. Workstations around the world could be automatically pressed into service. Imagine the dismay of a CEO who discovers that her new Whizbang 4200+ has been helping compute results for a competitor. Or imagine the legal ramifications in store for the owner of a government machine that inadvertently helps a foreign national break an encryption algorithm. Or imagine a computer hardware manufacturer who specs out a competitor's machine using a stealthy benchmark applet. The possibilities are many.

Forging Mail

Many Net-savvy UNIX users are aware of a simple trick allowing users to *forge* electronic mail. This is accomplished by talking directly to the **sendmail** daemon on port 25. The mail forging attack takes advantage of the fact that as an Internet standard, mail serving hosts are required to monitor port 25 for incoming *simple mail transport protocol* (SMTP) messages. Not only UNIX machines do this, but Windows95 and WindowsNT servers do the same thing. Non–mail-servers running Windows operating systems often use something called "POP mail." POP Mail clients are not subject to this attack.

One of the Internet *rites of passage* is to **telnet** to port 25, and send fake mail to a friend. This game is very well known. The scheme is easily debunked, though. The **sendmail** daemon actually marks the forged mail with the IP number of the machine that connected to port 25, which makes it very easy to discern which machine sent the mail.*

It is easy to detect forged mail by looking carefully at the header. The machine listed in the **From** line should be the same as the **Received:** line. Most users and mail readers look only at the **From** line. Systems people know to look at both. Here is an example of mail forged by an author on his home machine (**tigger.mediasoft.net**) to his own work account. Note how the **From** and **Received:** lines differ.

```
From god@heaven.edu Wed Jul 24 19:33:56 1996
Return-Path: <god@heaven.edu>
Received: from tigger.mediasoft.net by rstcorp.com (4.1/SMI-4.1)
id AA21199; Wed, 24 Jul 96 19:33:54 EDT
Received: from rstcorp.com
(gem@tigger.mediasoft.net[205.139.200.246])
by tigger.mediasoft.net (8.6.12/8.6.9) with SMTP id SAA00966
for gem@rstcorp.com; Wed, 24 Jul 1996 18:30:31 -0400
Date: Wed, 24 Jul 1996 18:30:31 -0400
From: god@heaven.edu
Message-Id: <199607242230.SAA00966@tigger.mediasoft.net>
Apparently-To: gem@rstcorp.com
Status: RO


This is forged mail.
```

---

* Of course on big university and corporate machines with hundreds of users, tracking down the actual person who originated the connection to port 25 may not be completely trivial. Dynamically assigned IP addresses also make finding out who forged mail hard.

Applets provide an interesting new twist on the standard approach to mail forging. Because applets load across the network and run on a Web surfer's machine, a mail forging applet can cause the standard **sendmail** daemon monitoring port 25 to report mail coming from the Web surfer's machine—not the machine serving the applet. This can be leveraged to *doubly forge* mail.

Imagine that someone hits a Web page and an applet is consequently run on the client machine. By using the victim's machine to forge mail from the victim—that is, to forge mail apparently both from the victim's machine and from the victim's account—the doubly forged mail will appear not to have been forged at all! With many standard configurations of **sendmail**, this forging attack is possible. Figure 4.4 illustrates the difference between the standard port 25 attack and the revised applet attack.

Forged mail of this sort can be sent to *any e-mail address* that the applet's author chooses. The message could, of course, be anything at all. To make this more concrete, imagine an applet that sends an e-mail death threat to the president of the United States (a felony) from the account and machine of anyone naive enough to browse a malicious Web page with Java enabled. Or, imagine an applet that uses mail to *spam* the **Usenet newsgroups** with a fake legal advertisement apparently posted from the victim's machine and account, immediately spawning a *mail bomb* attack against the applet's victim from angry **Usenet** users bent on retaliation. There are many variations on this theme.

Using threads, it is possible to forge mail in the background while doing something seemingly innocuous in the foreground. This forging activity is currently possible. In fact, there are multiple examples to be found on the Web. The possibly surprising fact is that the attack we have described is completely within the security bounds of what SMTP and Java are allowed to do. Forging mail like this is neither particularly sophisticated nor hard to implement. On the other hand, the havoc that could be wreaked with a malicious applet of this sort is serious.

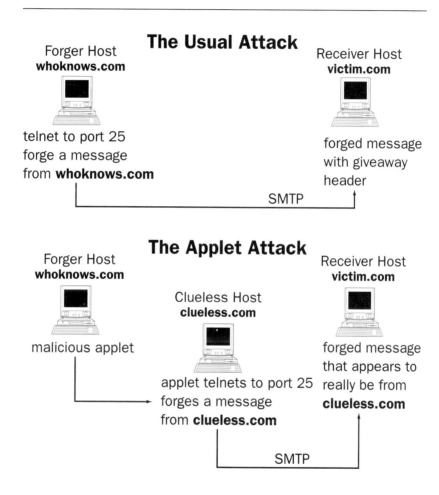

Figure 4.4 The usual mail forging approach versus the applet based **sendmail** approach. Because an applet runs on another host, it is possible to *doubly forge* mail so the resulting message does not appear to be forged.

Killing Off the Competition

The Business Assassin applet discussed earlier combines two dirty tricks. The first trick is to spawn a monitoring thread to watch for applets from another site. The second trick is to kill the threads of any incoming applets. According to the rules, an applet should not be allowed to kill the threads of other applets. Unfortunately what should not be allowed to happen and what actually can happen are not always the same. An implementation bug in the security check for thread access currently allows downloaded applets to access threads outside their own thread group.

Killing a thread is easy. Here is a code fragment that does it:

```
private static void ThreadMurder(Thread t){
        t.stop();
}
```

You may wonder why the **t.stop()** method is inside the **ThreadMurder()** method. This code will kill *any* thread **t**. It would be wise for the thread calling **ThreadMurder()** not to kill itself. Adding a test inside **ThreadMurder()** is an obvious way to do this. All that is needed is a simple name check. If the thread turns out to be checking itself, a decision is made to do nothing.

To make an applet that kills all threads not belonging to itself requires a bit more work. For clarity, lets call this applet **AssassinApplet**. A recursive approach to **AssassinApplet** is probably best. The basic outline:

1. Starting with the current thread group, ascend to the root thread group.
2. From the root, recursively descend through all threads and thread groups below.
3. Kill each thread encountered (but not self).

This is a very nasty and very effective approach.

If coded as above, an **AssasinApplet** would be able to kill all other applets running when it starts (a nice way to shut the **NoisyApplet** up!). It would also kill all applets that it comes across after that. Since it is possible within our framework for the applet to name who should not be killed, the **AssassinApplet** could run in tandem with other chosen applets. In fact, using the **AssassinApplet** at all times is an alternative to turning Java off! Just run the **AssassinApplet** once at the beginning of a session and after that all applets encountered from then on are guaranteed to be killed soon after arrival.

The Implications

Unlike the technically adept attacks of Chapter 3, these malicious applets are very easy to write. There are malicious applets that play background sounds endlessly. There are malicious applets that consume system resources, implementing denial of service attacks. There are applets that forge electronic mail. There are even applets that kill other applets' threads.

Now that techniques are widely available on the Hostile Applets Home Page (among other places), it is only a matter of time before malicious applets spread. Now that malicious applet source code has been put on the Web, hundreds of people will start to use and adapt the ideas. As we have seen, an applet need not break into your machine in order to perform maliciously. Sometimes it is good enough to steal CPU cycles, or deny access to other sites. Malicious applets come in all shapes and sizes. Defending against all of the possibilities is at best a daunting task.

Malicious applets may even play a role in undermining business on the Net. Recall the Business Assassin applet that targets Gamelan. Other anti-business applets might send forged mail with thousands of legitimate-seeming orders (resulting in thousands of expensive returns). Another malicious applet could spam the Net with ads supposedly from you, should you be from the site of a competitor. This could effectively cut your business off the Net when people respond with mail bombs. It does not take too much foresight to fear the implications that these applets have for Net commerce.

At least for the moment, malicious applets are not widespread. It is only a matter of time before they are. Now is the time to look into ways to defend ourselves against them. Sun Microsystems agrees: "We recognize the importance of providing people with some mechanism to help them deal with hostile applets." The next chapter will discuss a few possible ways the Java security model can be enhanced to address malicious applets. Some of the best ideas involve providing more effective means for controlling applets and threads, as well as monitoring and restricting access to system resources. Until then, it's *browser beware.*

Chapter 5

Antidotes and Guidelines for Java Users
Making Java more secure

Now that we've covered hostile applets, let's turn to the positive side and talk about what can be done to improve Java's security. Of course, security can always be improved by fixing specific bugs, as Sun Microsystems, Netscape, and Microsoft have been doing. Again, removing a needle from a haystack is easy once you've been stuck. This chapter focuses on more global issues surrounding the design of Java. What sorts of high-level antidotes are there to some of Java's security concerns?

This chapter has two major goals. The first goal is to discuss high-level concerns about Java and to make some suggestions about how they could be addressed. The second goal is to create a set of security guidelines Java users should follow. The high-level concerns include: programming language issues, formal analysis, applet logging, trust models, the distributed nature of the security model, implementation versus specification, decompilation, and trusted dialogs. Fixing the way that Java does some of these things will certainly improve security.

By establishing security guidelines, you can avoid most of the risks discussed so far. Many of these guidelines have been touched on in other chapters, here they will be consolidated in a complete package.

General Concerns and Their Antidotes

Most problems discussed in Chapters 3 and 4 involve specific vulnerabilities that have more to do with the current implementation of Java than with the Java security model itself. There are, however, some general concerns raised by the computer security community regarding Java. This section discusses some of these concerns and how addressing them would improve Java security.

Language Issues

The first group of issues has to do with the design of Java itself. There are three main language issues to discuss. Note that these are criticisms of the language itself, and not criticisms of the current implementation. It may be too late to address these concerns now that the Java ball is rolling, but these issues still warrant discussion.

Public Variables First among the language concerns is the fact that Java allows a kind of variable called a **public** variable. These variables can be overwritten by a method from any Java class, no matter where the class may have been defined, or from where that class may have been loaded. Storing any data in a public variable introduces a security risk.

In the current implementation, public variables are writable across name spaces. This means that a public variable can be overwritten by an applet that has come across the network. The global nature of public variables opens an entire avenue of attacks.

Packages A second language issue involves Java's **package** mechanism. Basically, packages in Java are too weak. A variable or method can be declared as accessible to classes within the current package, but there is no alternative way to control what sorts of other classes can access the variable. It would be better to have more explicit control over who can access variables. The flexibility to choose two of these classes, those four, and one from that other package to make up a new package would make the modularity mechanism much more versatile.

Consider the following statement: the **java.io.File** class is dangerous, and applets have no business accessing it. However, the same I/O class is required by code in **java.lang.ClassLoader** in order for the Class Loader to load classes from the local disk. Since **java.io.File** is needed outside its package, it must be declared public, making it accessible to applets. But making it public introduces a serious security hole. The hole can be plugged by adding a few rules (some code) to the Security Manager. As the Security Manager is built by the browser vendor (or some other Java application writer), such a solution is not very reasonable.

It would be better to have some way for **java.io.File** to be accessible to the **java.io** and **java.lang** packages, but not to any other code. This could be done; creating a stronger package system in Java.

In addition, the way membership in a package is declared is somewhat strange in Java. Most languages with package-like modularity, contain a single file outlining module declarations and lists of who is allowed to access the module. The owner of a module can then easily control who is allowed to use it. In Java, there is no single declaration of a module, or a list of members having access to the module. Instead, each class declares which package it belongs to, *itself*. That means that an external mechanism (such as the Security Manager) must decide whether or not untrusted code should be allowed to declare itself a member of a particular package. Because the package system is more complex than it needs to be, there is more room for error than with a more typical setup.

Byte Code Representation The next programming language critique is more abstract. Java's implementation of byte code is not optimal. As an intermediate representation between the Java source and the machine code of the platform Java runs on, byte code plays an important role. We believe there are better ways to represent the same sort of platform-independent code.

One construct, called Abstract Syntax Trees (AST), would be easier to type check than existing Java byte code. ASTs would replace the need for global dataflow analysis, which would speed up the Verifier. That's because ASTs have the same sort of information built directly in to them. ASTs also have the same semantics as the source languages they represent. That means there is no need to question whether the intermediate representation is more powerful than the source language. By contrast, Java byte code semantics are completely different from Java source code semantics. Who can guarantee that Java byte code is constrained in similar ways to the Java language itself?

If you're at a loss imagining why that matters, consider that some aspects of Java security depend on Java's semantics, and not on byte code semantics. Does that mean it may be possible to do things directly in byte code that a Java compiler would, for security reasons, not allow? Unfortunately, the answer is yes. For detail on this issue, see page 129. In any event, since ASTs have a compilation speed (source to AST) comparable to byte code compilation speed (source to byte code), why not use ASTs?

These and other language issues are discussed in greater detail in the Safe Internet Programming team's well-known IEEE paper "Java Security: From HotJava to Netscape and Beyond" [Dean et al., 1996]. If you are interested in learning more about such things, the article is available on the Web at URL **http://www.cs.princeton.edu/sip/pub/secure96 .html.**

Can Java Be Proven?

The discussion of ASTs and the current byte code representation leads directly to the next topic: formal verification. That's because any questions of provability are compounded by having two languages with separate semantics to understand (Java source and Java byte code). Formal verification involves proving, in much the same way that a theorem is proven in mathematics, that a program does what it is supposed to do. This is a laborious process, to say the least.

There are many sorts of formal analysis Java could undergo. The security model itself (if formalized) could be analyzed. The Java source language could be formalized in a specification, then shown to be valid. The same thing could be done for Java byte code. In addition, a better-specified formal relationship between Java byte code and Java source code could be worked out. The Java VM could also be formally verified. The security community will likely begin some of these analyses soon.

Formalizing the Security Model As briefly mentioned in Chapter 2, Java has no *formal* security model. The complete security policy has never been specified at a sufficiently high level. As a group of IEEE security researchers once said, "A program that has not been specified cannot be incorrect; it can only be surprising" [Young et al., 1995]. It is not possible to determine just what secure means without a creating a formalized policy. Furthermore, a particular implementation of a non–existent policy cannot be properly verified.

Analyzing Java Source The Java source language is powerful and includes a whole host of features. Only recently has any sort of specification of the language appeared. Given a complete specification of Java source semantics, a formal analysis can be completed. This work is currently underway.

Analyzing Byte Code Java byte code plays a critical role in the way Java works. Unfortunately, there is currently no specification for byte code semantics. This means that proving the Verifier and the VM work properly is not possible.

Comparing Byte Code and Java Source Showing how Java byte code behaves in relation to Java source code is also impossible without a semantics for both. It would be interesting to determine whether or not byte code is more powerful than Java source code. Are there things that you can do with byte code that you can't do through Java source? The answer seems to be yes. The Princeton team has discovered at least one instance in which it is possible to create byte code for an activity that is not allowed when going through the Java compiler. This suggests a new kind of Java cracker—a byte code bandit.

Analyzing the Java VM One problem affecting formal analysis of Java is the size of the Java system. With around 28,000 lines of code, Java raises critical assurance flags. Making certain that 28,000 lines of code do not introduce subtle vulnerabilities requires significant security analysis. No such analysis has yet been performed.

It is beyond today's technical capability to formally verify any piece of code in excess of 1,000 lines. This means that because of its size, Java is not amenable to formal proof of correctness. However, it may well be worth the effort to formally prove some aspects of Java correct. The first targets should probably be the VM and other security-critical pieces of the JDK, such as Class Loaders and Security Managers.

Software Engineering Many bugs have been found in various sections of the Java code. It is unlikely that security-critical code is bug free. Security vulnerabilities are often the result of buggy software. It is difficult enough to deal with bugs in standard code; bugs in security-critical code are much more serious.

This problem requires sound software engineering. That Java programs will be built out of pre-fabricated components will make any security bugs much more serious. Many different sites may end up using such a component that turns out to have a security problem. Not only will people liberally borrow security-impaired code snippets from each other, they will also begin to re-use entire classes of flawed code. Such code flaws will be increasingly difficult to isolate. Perhaps software engineering will develop a new approach which avoids such potential pitfalls. In any case, Java will continue to have an effect on what the future deems *state of the art*.

To Log or Not to Log

The next concern involves something very simple: keeping track of what Java does on your machine. One universal capability computer security experts rely on, no matter what the platform involved, is logging. Often the only way to reconstruct an intrusion is to carefully and painstakingly read the associated log files. Of course, such detective work is not possible in an environment lacking log files. Logs provide several benefits.

1. They allow the victim to determine what damage was done.
2. They provide clues about how to prevent similar attacks.
3. They provide evidence for possible legal or administrative proceedings against the perpetrator.

Java has no logging capability. It is possible to track neither which applets were loaded and run nor what those applets might have done. The most fundamental things that should be logged are file system and network access. Simply capturing this data would give system and security managers a chance to see what sorts of access were involved in an intrusion. File system access alone would help system managers protect files that Java crackers were accessing in their break-in attempts. It would also be good to capture applet byte code for analysis in case an applet ends up doing something hostile. It is often easier to recover from an intrusion if you know what caused it and what happened during the event.

Chapter 4 examined how an applet can delay its processing until a later time. Given that applets can do this, logging becomes even more important. An especially crafty malicious applet can wait until some other Web site becomes the main suspect before doing its dirty work. It won't be surprising if the most malicious applets turn out to be the craftiest. Tracking byte code would give system managers the ability to at least verify the function of each applet that may have been involved in an attack.

One of the lessons emphasized in *Takedown* is that without a log file it is impossible to prosecute computer criminals [Shimomura and Markoff, 1996]. Without a log file, you have no legal recourse in the event of a system break-in. If your site were hit by an attack applet today, erasing critical information, you couldn't do anything about it, even if you knew the culprit. Applet logging is an essential security feature that should be made available immediately.

Who Do You Trust?

Another notion common in computer security is the web of trust. If you know you trust someone (or some site), and you can safely authenticate their identity, then perhaps some of the more paranoid applet security measures can be relaxed. For example, companies on the Net may want to do applet-based business with companies they trust. Electronic Data Interchange (EDI) is an example of such a relationship.

Java currently has no built-in primitives for the required security infrastructure that might allow a web of trust to be set up. Encryption-based authentication and digitally-signed applets would be required for any serious application of sensitive data exchange. Chapter 6 discusses some of the concepts likely to show up in Java as soon as JDK 1.1.

Scattershot Security

One of the most common criticisms of the current Java security model centers on how Java spreads security functionality throughout the code. This means that security depends on many different parts working properly together. There is no centralized security system; no single source for security approval. Java implements security features through dynamic type checking, byte code verification, class loading restrictions, and run-time checks performed by the Security Manager. Each resides in a different part of the Java environment. Such a model depends on too many unrelated functions. If all of the security-critical functions were collected together in one place, that aggregate code could be more easily verified and analyzed. That simple step would satisfy some concerns held by security experts.

Some of Java's security policies are dependent on the Java language itself. This is fine if all Java byte code must be created by a Java compiler. But what guarantees does anyone have that byte code has been generated by a Java compiler that *plays by the rules*? There are none, nor should there ever be. There are compilers now in existence that turn Ada and C code into Java byte code. To take such third-party byte code development efforts away by legislating a particular compiler would go against the spirit of the language.

The problem is that the Virtual Machine interpreting Java byte code may allow more functionality than it should. More explicitly, there may be more functionality built in to the byte code than security would dictate. If the Java compiler never creates byte code capable of exploiting such features of the VM, then the architecture would seem to remain safe. Since nobody has control over who and what creates Java byte code, system managers should not rely on such a false hope. Someone could write a compiler able to create byte code that seems valid to the VM, but breaks rules ordinarily enforced by the Java compiler. See Figure 5.1.

One somewhat inefficient (but interesting) solution to this problem has been suggested by Andrew Appel of Princeton. He suggests checking byte code by first decompiling it to Java source, then recompiling the source to byte code. If a compiler you trust does not complain during re-compilation, then the original byte code is secure from the perspective of Java source. This process is slow, but sometimes it pays to be paranoid.

Formal analysis of the two languages and their relationship would also address this concern. The first steps in this process involve writing specifications for each language. We have heard that such an effort is currently underway. A formal analysis can tell us just what byte code could do that Java could not.

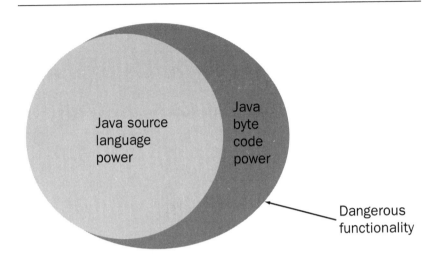

Figure 5.1 If Java byte code is more powerful than Java source code, then the extra functionality in byte code is dangerous. There is some evidence that this is the case.

Meeting the Specification

As a result of the successful line of Class Loader attacks described in Chapter 3, a helpful change was made to the Java specification. The fairly-subtle change involves the way the Java Virtual Machine interacts with Class Loaders.

Recall that the Java VM consults Class Loaders to help the VM determine which class names correspond to which real classes. Whenever the VM needs to know how to translate a class name, it asks the relevant Class Loader. If the VM needs to translate the same class name more than once, it asks the Class Loader each time. The Class Loader attack we described in Chapter 3 used an evil Class Loader that answered the same question in different ways at different times.

In order to prevent such attacks, the new Java specification decrees that the VM must remember the answers given by each Class Loader. When the VM needs the answer to a question is has already asked, it is required to reuse the answer given the first time rather than asking again. This new strategy is implemented in version 1.1 of the Java Development Kit.

Decompiling Java Byte Code

Although decompilation is not a traditional concern of security experts, it does have some interesting twists in Java. It turns out that one of the side-effects of Java byte code's clarity is that byte code is very easy to decompile. This means that given a **.class** file, it is possible to reconstruct reasonable source code automatically.

The JDK comes with a weak decompiler as one of its standard tools. Much better decompilers are available on the Web. The best we have seen is the "Mocha" Java decompiler, by Hanpeter van Vliet. The Mocha decompiler was once obtainable via URL **http://web.inter.nl.net/ users/H.P.van.Vliet/mocha.htm**. Recently, under pressure from Java developers, van Vliet removed Mocha from the Web. It may return. You can check on the status by visiting the Mocha Web site. Mocha's output is good enough to enable its users to understand and to modify a Java program, given only a **.class** file.

This is only relevant to security for a couple of reasons. The first reason is that businesses interested in using Java as a development language will need to consider the existence of decompilers before they distribute Java **.class** files. It probably won't be possible to sell something if making knock-offs turns out to be incredibly easy. Fortunately, van Vliet also intends to distribute a Java source code obfuscator. The end result of obfuscation is that though a **.class** file will decompile into valid Java, that valid Java won't be very readable by humans.

There is a second security concern related to decompilation. Given a piece of Java source code obtained by decompilation, a cracker can better analyze the program for weaknesses that could be exploited to break it. This would allow an attacker to intelligently attack a Java program (including applications such as Netscape's Java VM). Furthermore, an attacker could build a very realistic Trojan Horse program that looks almost exactly like the original. Like its ancient counterpart, a modern Trojan Horse is a program that appears to be one thing at one level but turns out to exploit security at another. Source code obfuscation would go a long way towards alleviating the concerns we have about decompilation.

Trusted Dialogs and Meters

In an earlier chapter, we raised the idea of providing trusted dialog boxes for critical actions like file I/O or critical measurements such as CPU cycles used. These dialogs would provide an important monitoring and feedback mechanism to Java users.

Providing a trusted set of dialogs (that cannot be spoofed) for things like file access seems like a good idea. However, with any such user interface one of the key goals must be to minimize user involvement in security. Most users don't read their dialogue boxes before they click *OK*. Sophisticated users should probably have some control over their security policies, but the less intrusive this control is the better.

Far from being in the way, a set of resource access indicators that cannot be forged would be a welcome addition to Java from nearly every user's perspective. This set of instruments could allow a user to track system resources such as CPU cycles, or microphone use. Such an indicator might go even farther and provide a way to kill errant or suspicious applets.

Java Antidotes

As can be seen from the laundry list of high-level concerns, Java security can be improved in many ways. Some of the most effective antidotes to Java security problems involve addressing the criticisms raised here. Look to Chapter 6 to see which ones are already close to release.

Guidelines for Java Users

It is all well and good to talk about what can be done to improve the next version of Java. But what about now? Are there guidelines for safely using Java as it exists today?

There are several straightforward things you can do to make your use of Java safer. Most of these are based on good old-fashioned common sense. Others require a bit of knowledge about Java. We have compiled a set of guidelines from the other chapters and organized them here.

- Know what Web sites you are visiting
- Know your Java environment
- Use up-to-date browsers with the latest security updates
- Keep a lookout for security alerts
- Apply drastic measures if your information is truly critical
- Assess your risks

Know What Web Sites You Are Visiting

The first piece of advice we have is of the common sense variety. Know what sorts of sites you are visiting with your Web browser. The chances of being attacked by an applet from a large corporate site like **sun.com** are very minimal. The chances of suffering an attack while surfing an underground cracker Web page are, of course, much greater.

You can avoid risk-laden Web sites by employing the same strategy you would use when visiting a big city. Use your intuition to continually assess your environment when you surf. If you are tempted to visit some cracker Web sites, do so with Java turned off. (Actually, make sure that all types of executable content are disabled when visiting such sites!)

Depending on your level of paranoia, you might consider all unknown Web sites as risky locations. A good strategy might be to leave Java off by default and turn it on only when you make a conscious decision to trust a site. Many business sites require that their employees use Java this way. This strategy is easy to implement. We discussed how to disable and enable Java on two popular browsers in Chapter 4.

Know Your Java Environment

Another piece of common sense advice is to know about the Java tools that you are using. Know how Java works (this book should help). Now that you know how Java treats built-in classes (see Chapter 2), you know how important it is to consider carefully what classes you should promote to built-in status.

Built-in classes are allowed to bypass all security verification checks. Never put Java classes (or **.zip** archives of classes) in your CLASSPATH unless you fully trust the vendor that distributed them. Also be aware that any sub-directories under the directories in your CLASSPATH may be searched for a class as well. Know who built your Java libraries and tools.

Be aware of what Java version you are using. Several companies have licensed the right to produce Java development environments. Some will probably do a better job with security than others. If the Java VM is buggy, then Java security is compromised. By using a particular vendor's version of Java, you are trusting the security of your machine to them.

This is actually a general lesson that applies to many technologies. Browser plug-ins should be subject to similar scrutiny. So too should any executable binaries loaded from the Internet.

Use Up-to-Date Browsers with the Latest Security Updates

This guideline may be a bit counter-intuitive, but you should always use the latest version of your favorite browser—even if it is a beta version. Some of the security holes discussed in Chapter 3 have been fixed in the very latest versions of Netscape and Internet Explorer. For example, security holes discovered in July have been fixed in Netscape 3.0*β*6. Be aware that no new versions of the 2.0 release have been updated to fix bugs. This implies that the beta versions are more secure. Of course, beta versions may also have new bugs of their own.

Recall that though the Princeton Class Loader attack has been fixed for current versions of Netscape (see "Applets Running Wild" in Chapter 3), the problem persists in version 2.0. The same thing goes for the Jumping-the-Firewall attack. Counting on an old version of a browser for your security is probably not a good idea.

Use the next guideline to help determine which version of a browser you need to have. Then get it.

Keep a Lookout for Security Alerts

Every once in a while check the latest security information on Java. This book's companion Web site (**http://www.rstcorp.com/java-security .html**) is quite current, but you should also keep an eye on the Sun Microsystems official Java Security FAQ. Also, have someone in your organization (or someone in your group of friends) subscribe to the CERT Alert list.

If the CERT Coordination Center finds a security hole either particularly egregious or particularly popular among crackers, they will warn the community at large. To date, CERT has issued two security alerts about Java. Both were related to attacks found by the Princeton team. We have reprinted the alerts in Appendix B, where you will also find information about signing up for on-line delivery of CERT Alerts.

The CERT Alerts have the advantage of telling you the status of any security attacks and how to avoid them. For Java, this includes information about which browser versions are susceptible to a particular attack, and which versions have been patched.

More Drastic Measures

There are, of course, a couple of drastic measures that can be applied to lessen Java security risks. These both involve not using Java. These drastic alternatives are not called for unless your information is ultra-critical. If you determine that the risks described are simply too great for you to bear, you can implement these strategies.

Stopping Java at the Firewall Just recently, firewall vendors including Trusted Information Systems (TIS) have added the capability of stopping Java applets at the gate by using special firewall products. TIS's Gauntlet Internet Firewall blocks Java applets by parsing a Web page's HTML code as it arrives. This action is performed by the **http** proxy. HTML-parsing capability makes a firewall capable of blocking any HTML-related tag. Thus, the relevant proxy can cut out Java (by looking for the **<APPLET>** tag), Javascript, and even old HTML 2.0 tags that are deemed disallowed during setup. This strategy is useful only for HTML coming in through the proxy via HTTP. That means applets coming into the system in other ways (for example, through a secure socket layer (SSL) or via **ftp**) can still get through.

Another solution to the same problem might be to try to stop all files with a **.class** extension at the gate. Still another would be to scan all incoming binaries for the magic number each applet is required to have. The end result is the same—no applets are allowed past the firewall.

Stopping all applets at the firewall is a radical solution that gives up all the good things that Java has to offer. It may be a viable alternative for machines that require limited Web access but are considered too important to expose to any risk beyond that. Unfortunately, this strategy resembles throwing the baby out with the bath water.

Hiding under the Bed Believe it or not, there are strategies even more paranoid than blocking applets at the firewall. Some sites may have such sensitive information that they decide they can't afford to take any risks at all. These sites protect themselves by not even connecting to the Internet in the first place. Java risk is thoroughly countered by this strategy. But all of the benefits that come with being connected to the Internet are given up in return. Java's power and flexibility may still find room on such a company's Intranet, but there will certainly be fewer uses for Java.

What the Authors Do about Using Java

Besides writing books about Java security, and poking holes in the Java security model, the authors are Java users as well. We thought you might be interested in hearing about the Java use policies that we use ourselves. Not surprisingly, they differ. Felten's policy is to keep Java off when he is browsing the Web unless he determines that a site is trustworthy. That means that Felten uses Java only when he has consciously thought about who created the applets at a site and what they are likely to do. He is careful to disable Java before leaving a site.

McGraw uses a similar strategy at work, where arbitrary Java use is against company policy (though not strictly enforced). He turns Java on at work only when he knows where he is on the Web and what the applets are going to do. Ironically, RST has several applets on the company Web site (**http://www.rstcorp.com**) that people using particularly strict strategies may never see! Though RST develops software testing tools for Java, they have decided that some of the risks associated with Java warrant a fairly tight Java use policy.

At home, McGraw surfs the Web with Java enabled all the time. That's because he is not worried about someone trashing his Linux box. He decided that the chances of encountering an attack applet are very low, and even if something bad does happen he can re-build with not much trouble. McGraw backs his data up at home.

Assess Your Risks

The title of this last section is really a guideline too, but the topic is important enough to warrant a section of its own. In some sense, the entire purpose of this book is summed up by the phrase *assess your risks*. Our goal in writing this book is to make you aware of what is going on with Java security. That way, you can make an intelligent, informed decision about what to do.

Each organization and individual must create their own strategy for using Java. The way to do this is to take a long hard look at the risks incurred through Java use. If these risks turn out to be too much to bear, then you should probably reconsider being connected to the Internet itself! Using Java is risky, but really not much more risky than simply being on the Net.

Risk assessment involves understanding what it would mean if the data on your machine were made public, what it would mean if your machine were to stop functioning, and what it would mean if the performance of your machine were suddenly and seriously degraded. Risks will differ according to context. That means if you have more than one machine, it is likely that risk assessments for each one will differ.

An intelligent Java strategy can only be made after understanding what you have to lose. If the answer is nothing, then there is no reason to worry about Java. If the answer is the business, then perhaps a more comprehensive Java security policy should be put in place.

When you are considering your risks, make sure you don't discount the benefits of Java. Java is an exciting and interesting technology that has lots to offer. Try not to throw out the good with the bad.

Chapter 6

Tomorrow's Java Security
Coming soon
to a browser near you

Now that you have reached this chapter, you have learned many things about today's Java security model. One of the key lessons emphasized throughout the book is that the current Java security model is a complex collection of details, some of which have flaws. This makes Java security both hard to understand and hard to analyze. The people at Sun Microsystems realize that Java security needs improvement, and they are working hard to provide real solutions. This chapter is devoted to discussing both near-term and long-term solutions that will improve Java security.

As you read this chapter, keep in mind that the authors have discussed future plans often and in detail with the companies that are involved in Java, but can't speak for them. Remember that things discussed in this chapter are not written in stone. Companies always hesitate to make predictions about the future, because often some of the things that they say are construed as promises. This is especially true when they discuss things that may be two or three generations down the road. This chapter presents estimates of what may happen, but the authors are not psychics.

The JDK 1.1 may already be out when you read this. The new JDK includes many new security upgrades, including the long-awaited digital signature capability. The first portion of this chapter discusses the capabilities likely to be included in the JDK 1.1. Most of the improvements slated for that release will be in common use by the time you read this.

Work on Java security goes beyond JDK 1.1 improvements, however, and the more remote future will be discussed as well. Later in the chapter we will cover security enhancements that are currently on the drawing boards, and that should become available in 1997. We will also touch on a few issues that may not appear until after that.

Most of the improvements to the security model are being developed and tested by Sun Microsystems.* But Sun does not work in a vacuum. There are several security researchers outside of Sun (including the authors) who are working to improve Java security. Some of the external projects currently underway include:

- defining a complete specification of the security model
- building an enhanced version of the Security Manager to serve as a true reference monitor
- performing formal analysis on aspects of the Java security model.

Also of interest are particular Java applications that have key security implications. Such applications include things like electronic commerce (now being hyped under the name Java Wallet), better firewall policies for Java applets (based on authentication and trust models), and an API for designing application-level security policies. We will devote some space below to security-related applications as well.

---

* Keep in mind that whenever Sun Microsystems makes an official change to Java (and freezes it into a new JDK), Java licensees are required to follow suit.

Though Java security has flaws in its current state, new ideas are coming on-line soon. As these new ideas are fully implemented and move into common practice, even farther-reaching future plans will begin to take shape. This chapter examines both ideas that will soon be available, and ideas that will not bear fruit for some time. The purpose of this chapter is to let you know what to expect on the Java security front so that your attitude toward Java is well-informed and your Java use decisions can be made with the most up-to-date information in mind.

Improvements in the JDK 1.1

The next release of the JDK (version 1.1), is slated to occur in late Fall 1996. That JDK will include some improvements and changes to the Java security model. Fortunately, none of the things that you have learned thus far about Java security will be outdated or replaced; rather, the Java security situation will be improved through a process of enhancement and addition.

The plans for JDK 1.1 have been fundamentally influenced by United States federal government restrictions on the use of encryption technology. Originally, the JDK was to include strong encryption in the form of RSA public-key cryptography. These plans had to be scrapped.

The federal government considers strong encryption algorithms such as RSA munitions, and imposes strict controls on their export. Many powerful algorithms (including PGP, a popular version of public key encryption) found their way around the world years ago and onto off-shore Web sites. Strangely enough, it is not illegal to publish strong encryption algorithms in a book. It is only illegal to distribute them in executable electronic form. This is a classic case of closing the barn door after the horse is gone. We find the current U.S. anti-encryption policy misguided and silly.

Beyond the restriction of RSA, U.S. government policies have also strongly affected well-publicized plans for the upcoming "crypto API." It now seems unlikely that encryption capability and the secure socket layer (SSL) communications package (both explained later) will be included in JDK 1.1. One strategy often employed by companies who find themselves constrained by the U.S. anti-encryption laws is to release strong encryption technology "domestically." This restricts the use of such packages to within the United States. It is likely that Sun Microsystems will resort to domestic release and use for data encryption standard (DES) and a few other things. This capability is likely to be released as a JDK extension. Hopefully the technology released in the U.S. will be legally exportable in the near future.

The most important changes planned for the JDK are the addition of authentication and access-control mechanisms that rely on the use of cryptography. A crypto API has been in the works for some time now, and will be partially turned on in the next release. The API provides a toolkit of cryptography tools that developers can use in their applets. Slated for release are digital signing capability, a system for certificate-based authentication (using X.509), and possibly the first cut at an access control toolbox.

From this point forward, read this chapter as though JDK 1.1 and the domestic JDK extension were not split apart due to anti-encryption laws.

The Crypto API

A few parts of the entire crypto API will be released in JDK 1.1. The parts most likely included are one way hash functions and digital signature capability. DES encryption tools will only be released as an extension. The main thing lacking in both domestic U.S. and foreign cases is public-key RSA encryption. Sun Microsystems is trying to gain United States federal government approval to include stronger encryption capability now.

In any case, encryption tools and their mathematically-related cousins (such as digital signing) will change the way Java use policies are managed. Digital signatures, which will be discussed next, make it possible to authenticate an applet author, and potentially check the applet for tampering. If you decide to trust a particular person, you can set things up so that you automatically trust the applets that person writes. Better yet, if you trust some experts in the field who agree to approve applets based on their analysis, you can trust any applets that they sign as well. Digital signing paves the way for a true community of trust to develop. We think digital signing is important enough to warrant an entire section itself. See page 145.

The crypto API will include a couple of other capabilities. One-way hash functions provide a way to fingerprint an applet or data so that you can verify that it has not been changed since being created. Fingerprinting hash functions such as MD5 and SHA make distribution over the Net easier to swallow. If you are certain that a program you are downloading from the Net is the original program (and not a Trojan horse masquerading as the original), you will probably be more likely to use it. Many archives on the Web make use of MD5 today. The crypto API will provide a way for applets to include this functionality.

Another function that should appear as part of the crypto API (at least in the U.S. extension) is DES encryption. DES is a kind of encryption that can in some cases be deciphered (given enough effort and a small enough key). DES is certainly much more secure than plain text, but does not provide the best available security. Most UNIX machines use a version of DES to encrypt user passwords stored in the **/etc/passwd** file. If 40-bit (or smaller) keys are used for DES, then the government will allow its export and use outside the United States. However, 40-bit keys are too small and provide only limited security from decryption. Most people use standard 56-bit keys. The ease of "breaking" DES is directly related to the length of its key.

As we mentioned above, the crypto API is also intended to include the much stronger RSA encryption algorithm. Export restrictions have put a hold on those plans, for now. The fact that RSA is not free software also complicates matters. RSA is a proprietary algorithm sold by RSA Data Security, Inc. (**http://www.rsa.com**). Since Java is currently distributed by Sun Microsystems free of charge, it is not clear that

RSA will allow their technology to be bundled with Java in such a way that it can be redistributed by others. If these two issues can be resolved by 1997, you may expect to see RSA appear in the crypto API then.

Certificates

A feature reminiscent of Netscape that will appear in JDK 1.1 is certificate technology based on the X.509v3 open standard. Certificates provide an authentication mechanism by which one site can securely recognize another. Sites that recognize each other have an opportunity to trust each other as well. When a secure socket layer (SSL) connection initializes, they handshake by exchanging certificates. SSL is discussed on page 155.

A certificate is a piece of identification (credential) much like a driver's license. Information stored inside a typical certificate file includes the subject's name, the subject's public key, the certificate's issuer, the issuer's digital signature, an expiration date, and a serial number.

So the question is, who gives out these certificates? Somebody (or some thing) called a certification authority (CA). There are a handful of companies that have set themselves up as CAs in the world. These include: Netscape, GTE, Verisign, and a few others. But why should you trust them? Good question. (See page 149.)

Access Control

The last thing likely to show up in the JDK 1.1 is a set of access control hooks that can be made available to a server. Access control lists (or ACLs) aid in the formation of security policies. The HotJava browser (first released with Java in 1995 and since disappeared off the radar screen) allowed for the specification of fairly complex ACLs by a user. It is not clear that any ACL functionality will be made available to end-users of Java in JDK 1.1, but a rudimentary ACL toolbox will probably be part of the release.

As with the RSA/crypto API situation, a more mature version of ACL will probably be held off until sometime in 1997. This version will include stronger authentication mechanisms and will enhance the ability of server users to define more complex security policies.

Signed Applets

The capability to digitally sign applets is finally near release. The JDK 1.1 should be out soon if it isn't already. Digital signing capability is an important part of the much-ballyhooed crypto API. This is exciting because digital signing will radically alter the amount of trust you can place in an applet.

One particular kind of cryptography tool allows a chunk of digital information (including, of course, Java byte code) to be signed by its authors or distributors. Because a digital signature has special mathematical properties, it is irrevocable and unforgeable. Your browser can verify a signature, allowing you to be absolutely certain of that applet's origin. Better yet, you can instruct your browser always to accept applets signed by some party that you trust, or always to reject applets signed by some party that you don't trust.

It is important to recognize that even if you know exactly which Web pages you are visiting and who created them, you probably don't know who wrote each applet that appears on the pages you visit. Applets are shuffled around on the Net like baseball cards in a fifth-grade classroom. Furthermore, it is not always clear that you are visiting the site you think you're visiting.

Contrary to popular belief, you don't always know where information is coming from on the Internet. A nasty attack called IP spoofing allows a bad guy to send you network traffic that claims to come from someplace else. For instance, you might think the traffic is coming from **whitehouse.gov**, when it's really coming from **cracker.org**. IP spoofing used to be considered just a theoretical possibility, but it has actually happened in recent years. The best known example is an attack by the infamous cracker Kevin Mitnick on a machine managed by computer security worker Tsutomu Shimomura. Mitnick's attack led to his eventual capture and conviction.

Even if you ignore the possibility of IP spoofing, using the return address of an applet (that is, knowing the Web site where you got the applet) still isn't good enough. A digital signature holds much more information. For example, such a signature could tell you that though the applet is being redistributed by a site you don't trust, it was originally written by someone you do trust. Or it can tell you that although the applet was written and distributed by somebody you don't know, your friend has signed the applet, attesting that it is safe. Or perhaps it can simply tell you which of the thousands of users at **aol.com** wrote the applet.

Digital Signatures

So how do you sign an applet? The key to certification and authentication is the use of digital signatures. The idea is simple: to provide a way for people to sign electronic documents so that these signatures can be used in the same way we use signatures on paper documents. In order to be useful, a digital signature should satisfy five properties [Schneier, 1995]. It should be:

1. *Verifiable*: Anybody should be able to validate a signature.
2. *Unforgeable*: It should be impossible for anybody but you to attach your signature to a document.
3. *Non-reusable*: It should be impossible to "lift" a signature off one document and attach it to another.
4. *Unalterable*: It should be impossible for anybody to change the document after it has been signed.
5. *Non-deniable*: It should be impossible for the signer to disavow the signature once it is created.

Mathematicians and computer scientists have devised several digital signature schemes that work quite well. The full details are very technical. If you're interested in learning more about such schemes, Bruce Schneier's book, *Applied Cryptography*, is a good place to start learning about the subject.

The digital signatures used for Java code are based on *public-key cryptography*. If Alice wants to be able to sign documents, she must first use a special mathematical technique to generate two large numbers: her own *private key*, and her *public key*. As the names suggest, Alice keeps her private key to herself. Keeping it secret is essential. Her public key, though, she announces to the world.

Alice's private key is used for signing electronic documents. Her public key is used to verify those signatures. Anybody who knows the private key (hopefully only Alice!) can run a special computation involving the document and Alice's private key. The result of this process is a digitally signed version of the document.

Anybody who knows Alice's public key can verify her signature by running a special computation involving the signed document and Alice's public key. Since only Alice knows the private key, she is the only one who can put her signature on documents. Since everybody knows her public key, anybody can verify that the signature is hers.

Everything sounds great. You tell your browser to trust applets signed by Alice by registering Alice's public key. Whenever applets claim to come from Alice, the browser can verify that claim by comparing the registered public key to the signed applet. If the applet is not from Alice, it can be rejected.

Key Distribution

But how does one know what Alice's public key is?

If you know Alice, she can call you on the phone and tell you her public key. In this case, you will know the key is valid because you recognize Alice's voice. This doesn't work if you don't know Alice. How do you know the person on the other end of the phone is Alice? Maybe it's Alice's evil twin Zelda, trying to pass off Zelda's public key as Alice's so she can forge Alice's signature.

One way around this problem is to ask Alice's twin brother Allan to help. Alice can create a document containing her public key and have Allan sign that document. If you trust Allan and you know Allan's public key, then the document tells you reliably what Alice's public key is.

But how do you know Allan's public key? You can't ask Alice and Allan to vouch for each other's public keys, because Zelda could create a false Alice key *and* a false Allan key and use them to sign documents vouching for each other! This leaves us stuck with a chicken-and-egg problem.

The usual solution is to use a *certification authority* (CA). The CA, Claire in our example, is in the business of certifying keys. Alice goes to the CA's office with her birth certificate, passport, driver's license, and DNA sample. Once she has convinced Claire that she really is Alice, she tells Claire her public key, and Claire signs an electronic document that contains Alice's public key. That document serves as an electronic credential for Alice.

After Alice has a credential, key distribution is much easier. Alice can plaster copies of her credential everywhere: on bulletin boards, on her home page, and at the end of every e-mail message she sends. Better yet, whenever Alice signs a document, she can attach a copy of her credential to the signed document. On receiving the document, you can first check the credential by verifying Claire's signature, and then verify Alice's signature using the public key included with the document. Zelda can't trick you into accepting a bogus public key for Alice, because she can't forge Claire's signature.

The beauty of this approach is that if everybody can visit Claire and get a credential, then nobody has to remember any keys except for their own private key (so they can sign documents), and Claire's public key (so they can verify credentials). There are still two problems, though. Everybody must trust Claire. As *the* authority, she can impersonate anybody. And you still need a reliable way to get Claire's public key. It doesn't help to have Claire get a credential from Claire's mom, Elena. You would have no more reliable way of knowing who Elena is.

There is no technological solution to this. Claire's key will probably be hard-wired into your browser software, or entered by support staff at install time. As long as you get a valid copy of the browser, and nobody has messed with your hard disk, everything will be OK. How do you know you have a valid copy of the browser? It will be signed by the browser vendor. How do you know the browser vendor's signature is valid? Don't ask—there lies madness.

What Signing Can't Do

Even if the signing and signature-checking mechanisms work perfectly, and are able to reveal who signed each applet, there is still a huge unsolved problem. Technology can tell you who signed an applet, but it can't tell you whether or not that person is trustworthy. That's a decision you have to make based on human judgment. And you'd better make the right decision.

Trust

Once a code signing infrastructure is in place, you will be able to know reliably who vouches for each applet. The next link in the chain is figuring out what to do with that knowledge.

One thing you can certainly do is to relax Java's security rules for applets that you trust. For example, Java normally prohibits any access to files in order to prevent an applet from corrupting your hard drive, or reading your private data. If you trust applets from a particular source, though, you might want to allow them to read files. Doing this opens up vast new application areas including things like spreadsheet applets, games with stored high scores, Web sites that recall your preferences, a host of different remote management possibilities, and so on.

Besides access to files, there are many other capabilities you might want to grant a trusted applet: access to your machine's microphone and camera, freedom to make network connections, and maybe even freedom to label other applets as trusted.It all depends on your decision to trust and how much to trust these applets. There are several ways you can make these decisions.

Whom Do You Trust?

The first decision is whether to use a black-and-white or a shades-of-gray policy. A black-and-white policy is one that divides all applets into two groups, trusted and untrusted. A shades-of-gray policy allows you to assign any degree of partial trust to an applet.

Before Java came along, most Internet software worked on a black-and-white model. If somebody offered to let you download a program, you had two choices: either you downloaded the program or you didn't. If you did, you were trusting the program completely since there was nothing to stop it from running wild on your machine. If you didn't download the program, you were treating it as completely untrusted. Java, with its security policies, changed the rules a bit by making it easier to decide which to download in the first place. If an applet can't bite you, you might as well check it out.

The black-and-white model is sometimes called the shrink-wrap model because it's similar to software you purchase. If you buy a software package from a reputable software store, you can reasonably assume that the software is safe to load onto your machine. People who use the term shrink-wrap model tend to assume that nobody would ever want to run software that wasn't written by a large software company. We don't agree with that implication, so we'll stick with the term black-and-white.

It might seem that the shades-of-gray model is better than the black-and-white model, because black-and-white only allows you to label applets as completely trusted or completely untrusted. On the other hand, shades-of-gray gives you more choices. You may still label an applet as completely trusted or completely untrusted if you wish.

Choices are not always good, as anybody who has encountered the cereal aisle of a large supermarket can attest. Making choices takes up time that you would probably rather spend doing something else. Frequent decision-making saps your attention span, so you are more likely to make a mistake, thus opening yourself up to attack. Finally, having more options saddles your browser with more complicated record-keeping duties to keep track of all of your decisions. This extra complexity might lead to bugs in the browser, possibly jeopardizing security yet again.

Which model is better, black-and-white or shades-of-gray? It depends on how people react to the two systems, which is hard to predict. Mostly likely, competing browsers will offer different models, and the models will fight it out in the marketplace. The decision is ultimately one of user preference.

Free the Trusted Applets!

Once you've decided who to trust, the next question is what you allow trusted applets to do. If you're using the black-and-white model, then you have to decide whether to allow untrusted applets to run at all. You also have to decide what extra capabilities, if any, you want to give to trusted applets. You might decide to let trusted applets do whatever they want, with no restrictions at all. Or you might decide to run trusted applets under today's restrictive Java security rules. The choices depend on your taste for risk, and what kinds of applets you want to run. With black-and-white security, though, all the applets you trust receive the same level of trust.

If you're using a shades-of-gray model, you face more choices. You may decide on an applet-by-applet (or author-by-author) basis exactly which capabilities to grant. Rather than presenting you with a huge laundry list of possible capabilities for each applet, and forcing you to tick items off the list, a good browser will probably provide a way for you to grant certain pre-packaged sets of capabilities. For example, there might be a set of permissions for video conferencing applets, which would include things like permission to use the camera, the microphone, the speaker, the display, and networking access. Perhaps there would be another set of document-editing applet permissions, which would include file-creation, file-reading, and file-modification capabilities.

An Outside Assessment of Java

Java security is important. If executable content is to take wing, people will first have to determine that the security situation is acceptable to them. Do Sun Microsystems, Netscape, and Microsoft have too much to lose to make an honest assessment of their own Java security models? Fortunately the answer to that question is irrelevant! There are several outside security agents involved in assessing the Java security model. It is important for objective third-party analysis of Java security to take place. Chapter 3 made that need quite plain.

Public Scrutiny

Java security gets a fair amount of public scrutiny. At least occasionally, the popular press is also involved. When the Princeton team discovered their two most-famous bugs (the Jumping-the-Firewall attack, and the Applets-Running-Wild attack), the news was picked up by many major newspapers including: *USA Today, The Wall Street Journal, The New York Times, The Boston Globe,* and *The Los Angeles Times* (just to name a few). Lately though, the discovery of new bugs has not made such an impact on popular media.

That doesn't mean that Java has become instantly secure. Nor does it mean that the newly-discovered bugs are any less serious than their now-famous ancestors. The new bugs are just as serious, but the novelty seems to have worn off. Contributing to the more sedate reaction in the press is another factor: the very reasonable and timely reactions of Sun Microsystems, Netscape, and Microsoft to the news of flaws in their security models. Lines of communication between the Princeton team and the three major Java players exist today that simply didn't exist before. That makes for better cooperation, and more importantly, it makes for better security.

Obviously, this book also contributes to the public scrutiny Java security receives. It is a good thing for people to be aware of the risks they are taking when they use the Web and the Net. It is also a good idea to learn as much as possible about how security on your machine really works. Informed users will tend to be safer users. The information in this book should be made available to everyone using Java-enabled browsers.

Outside Contractors

In addition to the authors, there are some outsiders who have been contracted by Sun Microsystems to help them work on improving Java security. These people are involved in a couple of important projects. The first such project is an analysis of the Java Security Reference Model, currently evolving from the Security Manager. This model will provide a more concrete understanding of how Java security should work. The model is intended not as a proper *formal model*, but as an English description. Eventually, a formal model and formal analysis of the reference model will be developed. Such an analysis will put to rest some of the high-level criticisms that Java security has been subject to (see Chapter 5). A good portion of the reference model analysis should be completed soon.

Another project underway that involves outsiders is the development of a formal specification (spec) of a good portion of the Java VM. It is not possible to determine with any accuracy whether or not any particular VM implementation is sound without writing such a spec first. Writing a spec is a good first step toward gaining a deeper understanding of the VM. A spec also provides a critical stepping stone along the way to a formal analysis of the security model. We hope that once the Java VM spec is completely developed it will be released to the rest of the Java community. A number of outside researchers will be able to help perform security analysis once such a spec is in place.

Whenever contractors are involved, there is always some question regarding how independent their analysis will remain. One way that Sun Microsystems can alleviate these concerns is to publish results of the two efforts discussed above. That way these important results will be subject to the public scrutiny they deserve.

For a Future JDK

The farther into the future the authors look, the less clear the picture. Nevertheless, it is important to prepare for some of the changes that might affect us.

Some of these new additions to the JDK will appear soon. If not in JDK 1.1, then in the next release. The most important of these additions is a completely finished crypto API, including DES and RSA encryption toolkits. The two issues holding encryption up are export control problems, and the proprietary nature of the RSA algorithms. These things should be worked out in 1997.

Also slated for a future JDK is a more complete version of access control lists (ACLs). They should include more mature authentication mechanisms. With ACLs in place, the way will be prepared for user-defined security policies—or at the very least, user-defined security policies for servers.

A third security mechanism being discussed for a future JDK is support for authentication protocols. The most famous such protocol is Kerberos, but it is somewhat messy and depends too much on a central server. Solutions for an authentication protocol are still being researched.

Securing Particular Java Applications

There are a number of projects underway at JavaSoft, the browser companies, and elsewhere that will require strong security. This section will cover some of them. First, we will make a short detour to cover secure communication.

Secure Communication

Some Java products released in the near future will include a package for secure socket layer (SSL) communication. Similar to Netscape's SSL, the Java SSL provides a secure communications channel by using encryption. SSL works by providing a mechanism for encrypting packets on the sending end, sending them over an untrusted channel, and decrypting them at the receiving end. SSL is useful for many business applications, including the transmission of proprietary information and electronic currency.

Most Web servers and browsers now support SSL, allowing a browser to communicate with a Web server without anybody else overhearing the conversation. (Well, an outsider might overhear a conversation, but they certainly won't understand it.) Though SSL is commonly used over the Web, it can actually be used to protect virtually any sort of network transaction.

Most browsers support SSL by providing a "Secure HTTP Connection" service that looks to the user just like a normal Web connection, but uses SSL underneath. This allows you to reap the benefits of SSL without having to learn anything except how the browser tells you whether a connection is secure. (Current implementations of SSL require *certificates* in order to work. Certificates, and their role in SSL, are explained on page 144.)

The encryption technology underlying SSL is believed to be secure, but there are two potential problems. First, the U.S. government restricts the export of strong cryptography software. If your browser version includes dumbed-down exportable cryptography software, your communications might not be as secure as you think. Second, SSL is good at providing secure communications, but it is not as good at establishing who you are communicating with. This leads into all the problems of authentication and key distribution discussed on page 147.

Java Applications

Many Java products have unique security needs that may or may not be built into the JDK. Security plays a key role in these products.

- *Java Wallet*—Electronic commerce requires strong security. Security features should include: 1.) authentication mechanisms (to ensure that customers, clients, and stores are who they say they are); 2.) secure communications like SSL (so that information like credit card numbers can be safely transferred over unprotected wires and privacy is guaranteed); and 3.) foolproof mechanisms for a new kind of electronic money. The Sun Microsystems team working on the Java Wallet is developing their own security mechanisms in addition to relying on those that are (or will soon be) built into Java. The Java Wallet team does intend to use the current JDK security API including parts of the domestic extension. But because they need more functionality, the Java Wallet team is developing their own internals. When money is involved, the standard for security is much higher. This suggests that for Java Wallet to catch on, detailed security analysis will be required. If Java itself is not secure, it is unlikely that Java Wallet will be either.

- *Firewall Tools*—As Java becomes even more pervasive, corporate users who rely on firewalls as a first line of defense are going to demand more Java policies built into their firewalls. These days, most firewall code is written in C. But the Java authentication mechanisms allowing for digital signatures will be implemented in Java. How will these things work together? People are just beginning to think through these question now. Stay tuned for solutions.

- *JavaBeans Components*—Chapter 1 introduced the idea of Java components, and a new kind of software engineering based on pre-fabricated Lego block-like compositions. There are several such models currently under development, including: CORBA, ActiveX, and JavaBeans. Obviously, building a Java program out of parts written by someone else is going to radically affect security. Making component-based security work promises to be a difficult problem in the current Java security model.

- *Persistent State*—Persistent state refers to a facility that allows Java programs to write arbitrary Java data structures to a file, and then later to reconstitute them from the file. This poses some security risks, since data structures sitting on the disk are vulnerable to snooping and modification. There is also the problem of version juggling: What happens if a data structure present in version 1.2 is written out by version 2.3, then reconstituted by version 4.0? If these issues are not dealt with very carefully, new opportunities for mischief will arise.

- *Remote Method Invocation*—JavaSoft is now offering an early version of their Remote Method Invocation (RMI) facility. This allows a Java program or applet running on one machine to call methods of Java objects that are part of another program, somewhere else on the Net. RMI offers the same problems as persistent state, since data structures must be written across the network and then reconstituted on arrival at the destination. There are also concerns about how data gets transmitted across the network. If the designers are not careful, there might be a way for an attacker to replay a previous call or to learn useful information by snooping on RMI messages.

- *Cross-Language Calls*—Both major browser vendors are offering ways for Java programs to interact with code written in other programming languages: Microsoft has ActiveX, and Netscape has LiveConnect. Problems might arise in cases where the security models of the two languages don't match. For example, ActiveX may assume that programs behave in a certain way while Java doesn't enforce that behavior. It's generally true in security that the more components are interacting, the more opportunities there are for things to go wrong.

- *JavaOS*—Sun Microsystems is working on JavaOS, a stand-alone operating system that can support Java programs and applets. The idea is that conventional, bulky operating systems such as Windows 95 are complete overkill for the needs of a browser. A small computing device could run the smaller and simpler JavaOS for users who don't need more than a browser. JavaOS would provide enough of a platform for Java programs to run. The security risks here lie in the very novelty of JavaOS. There are many security mistakes that JavaOS could make. Most existing operating systems have been well tested and debugged.

As the Java security model matures, and the JavaSoft security team gets better organized, they will play a key role in helping develop security policy for some of the applications listed here. It is crucial not to scatter parts of the Java security model any more than they are now.

The Distant Future

This section will go out on a limb to make predictions about what might occur more than two JDK generations from now. This is an estimate made by the authors who could well be wrong. Because of the fast-paced nature of the industry, anything past 1997 is incomprehensibly far in the future. Nevertheless, there are people at Sun Microsystems who are thinking about long-term security goals for Java. Who knows, some of these things might become so important that they show up tomorrow.

Not surprisingly, the concerns for the far future are fairly high level in nature. The first has to do with the way Java treats trusted and untrusted code. The current model (called the sandbox, for some reason) is to put untrusted Java code in its own little area away from everything else. All untrusted code enjoys the same level of complete suspicion. Thus the sandbox implements a black-and-white security policy. In the future, with the help of applet signing and authentication, the current black-and-white model will be expanded to include a ring of levels. In such a model, some applets could be trusted more than others. The farther in an applet gets, the less it is trusted. Applets that are completely untrusted (as is the case for all applets today) reside in the middle. You could call this the ring of distrust. The ring idea is one possible way to implement a shades-of-gray policy. There are, of course, many other ways to do this.

Also slated for research is a fundamental change to the way the access control list model works. The idea is to provide a safe and secure way to do remote method invocation (RMI). RMI will only be possible with a strong ACL system in place. The ACL model currently under development may not be up to the job. Even with a perfect system of ACLs in place, there are other hard security issues that will need to be dealt with in order to safely allow RMI.

The whole notion of component-based software has a long way to go before it is ready for market. Many researchers are interested in finding methods for improving and assessing component security and reliability issues. JavaBeans currently has no mechanisms for security assurance built-in (other than the standard JDK things, that is). That will have to change before JavaBeans gains widespread support.

The final future security goal to discuss is the idea of working security directly into the **Object** class itself. Making some fundamental changes to the root object will make it easier to solve some of the hardest security problems in Java. Since every Java class inherits characteristics from the **Object** class, a change made to that class would percolate throughout the entire Java language. Security researchers at Sun Microsystems are trying to understand what sorts of changes might be necessary, and what the implications for security would be.

Should You Use Java?

By now you should know the authors' answer to this important question: it depends. Though not entirely satisfactory, there is no way to properly make Java use decisions on anything other than a case-by-case basis. The way to make your own decision about Java is to start by assessing your risks. What could you lose? The next step is to weigh the risks against the benefits. Is what you gain worth the potential loss?

Java has lots to offer. It's the most viable attempt so far to provide executable content. Java is deeply tied to the Web and comes with many advanced networking features. Java is powerful and can be used to write full-fledged programs. Java is a more portable application language than any other on the market today. To top it off, Java is truly concerned with security.

On the other hand, by using Java you are taking risks. Security can never be completely guaranteed. Anybody who tells you it can is wrong. By connecting your computer to the Net at all, you have decided to take some degree of risk. If you're willing to do that, then you should probably be willing to use Java. Then again, there are things about Java that set it apart from other languages and Internet services. For one thing, Java makes running someone else's untrusted code a normal event!

The previous chapters have explained the current Java security model. Included in that discussion is an analysis of the vulnerabilities found thus far. Hostile applets—both in the serious *attack applet* guise and in the antagonistic *malicious applet* guise—are a possibility that needs to be taken seriously. Security research on Java will continue to expose problems in the future. The security community, working closely with Sun Microsystems, Netscape, and Microsoft will make sure each new vulnerability is quickly and properly patched.

In addition to discussing particular bugs in the current Java implementations, we have also examined some more general concerns. Hopefully, most of these will be addressed in the enhancements planned for the near future.

We hope this book will continue to prove a useful reference on Java security. Armed with this information, you can make informed decisions regarding your own Java use.

Appendix A

Java Security: Frequently Asked Questions

Here are the unofficial answers from the Princeton Safe Internet Programming team.

Is Java safe?

Nothing in life is completely safe; Java is no exception. Several specific security problems have been discovered and fixed since Java was first released. If you're using an up-to-date Web browser, you are usually safe from the known attacks. However, nobody is safe from attacks that haven't been discovered yet.

If somebody says Java is safe because "hackers aren't smart enough to exploit the problems," don't believe them. We're disappointed that some people who should know better are still spouting this nonsense. We've discovered several security problems, and we're pretty sure we're not the smartest people in the world. If one group of hackers creates a Java-based attack and shares it with their friends, we're all in trouble.

Other Web "scripting" tools such as JavaScript, Visual Basic Script, or ActiveX face the same sorts of problems as Java. "Plug-in" mechanisms provide no security protection. If you install a plug-in, you're trusting that plug-in to be harmless.

What are the risks?

There are two classes of security problems: nuisances and security breaches. A nuisance attack merely prevents you from getting your work done—for example, it may cause your computer to crash. Security breaches are more serious: your files could be deleted, your private data could be read, or a virus could infect your machine.

If you are the victim of a security breach, any data stored on your machine may be read or corrupted by a bad guy. If you've got important company secrets on your computer, maybe you should surf the Net on another machine.

In the not-too-distant future, your computer may be able to digitally sign documents that are legally binding, just like your paper signature. Your computer may also be able to spend your money. In a world like that, security becomes even more important than it is right now.

How common are security breaches?

So far, there have been no publicly reported cases of security breaches involving Java. Of course, this is no guarantee that there haven't been breaches that either weren't discovered or weren't reported. But it does indicate that breaches are rare.

Who is at risk?

You're at risk if you're running a Java-enabled browser and you visit a Web page written by a person you don't know or don't trust. Because the two most common browsers, Netscape Navigator and Microsoft Internet Explorer, are Java-enabled, most people surfing the Web are at risk.

How can I protect myself?

If you maintain sensitive data on your computer that you think an unscrupulous adversary might want, you should disable Java and JavaScript and avoid installing plug-ins, except those from well-known vendors.

If you don't disable Java, think twice before visiting a Web site belonging to a person you don't know or don't trust. Of course, some people will be perfectly happy just living with the risk.

You can reduce the damage caused by a potential security breach by taking common-sense precautions like backing up your data frequently and keeping sensitive data off your Web-surfing machine.

Won't digital signatures solve all of the problems?

No, they'll help only a little. Digital signatures let you know who wrote an applet, but they don't help you decide whether you can trust the author.

Is this problem ever going to go away?

No. Security will always be an issue with any network software. As long as vendors are racing their products out the door and adding new functionality with each and every release, you can expect that security bugs will always exist. Writing crash-proof software is hard. Writing secure software is even harder.

I'm a Netscape Navigator user.
Which version should I use?

Generally, the latest fully released version is the safest. Be sure to check Netscape's Web pages regularly for announcements of new versions. Look carefully—the announcements are not always prominent.

Okay, but what about Microsoft's
Internet Explorer?

Internet Explorer 3.0, currently in beta test, now supports Java. We are currently studying the security of Microsoft's Java implementation.

What about "black widows?"

There's a report circulating on the Net, claiming to come from the USGS, containing various misleading and inflammatory statements about Java security and using the term "black widows." Some statements attributed to us in that report are simply false. You can read our original paper and see for yourself.

What about "hostile applets?"

This is a general term for Java applets (programs) that exploit security bugs. Some pages on the Web demonstrate, with appropriate warning messages, some hostile applets. The applets we've seen are nuisance attacks rather than damaging attacks.

I run a Web server. Am I at risk?

Not directly. Java can potentially attack only the browser, not the server.

Of course, you should be careful about which Java applets appear on your server. Unless you wrote the applet yourself, you don't necessarily know what it's doing. If you copy somebody else's applet, it could possibly be a Trojan Horse—doing something useful as well as being malicious.

What about JavaScript?

Java and JavaScript, despite the similarity of their names, are not related. (Isn't marketing wonderful?) JavaScript has its own security problems, so you may also want to disable JavaScript.

What did your lawyers tell you to say?

This information is our opinion only. It is not the opinion of Princeton University or of our research sponsors. We do not and cannot guarantee that you will be safe if you follow our advice.

Where can I find more information?

JavaSoft has its own Frequently Asked Questions about Applet Security.

Netscape has a Netscape Navigator 2.02 Security-Related FAQ that you may find interesting. To see how Netscape plans to evolve its security model, you may want to read Netscape's Java Security Architecture.

Mark LaDue, at Georgia Tech, has a page of hostile applets to demonstrate how serious the problem can be.

David Hopwood, at Oxford University, has also been active in breaking Java.

Microsoft doesn't (yet) have a Java security FAQ, but you may want to read its proposals for code signing (part of its Internet Development Toolbox), or maybe "Dr. GUI Gets Webbed," for a more whimsical look at Microsoft's vision of the Web's future.

Safe Internet Programming

Princeton University

Department of Computer Science

Contact: sip@cs.princeton.edu

Last modified: Tuesday July 23, 1996.

CERT Alerts*

The CERT Coordination Center is a DARPA-funded organization that provides emergency assistance to people suffering from attacks on their computers. The CERT Web page is located at URL **http://www.cert.org**. One of the services that CERT provides is a series of alerts about especially important security vulnerabilities. The CERT alerts are broadcast to a mailing list of interested system administrators and security researchers. If you would like to add yourself to the mailing list, send a message to: **cert-advisory-request@cert.org**. CERT alerts are also archived on the CERT ftp site: **ftp://ftp.cert.org/pub**.

CERT has issued two security alerts dealing with Java security. They are numbered **CA-96.05.java_applet_security_manager** and **CA-96.07.java_bytecode_verifier**. Though CERT intends to change the way its alerts are updated in the near future, at present any new information relevant to an existing alert is appended to a README file of the same name as the original alert. Below, with the permission of the CERT Coordination Center, we include the full text of both Java-related security alerts and their associated READMEs.

★ Special permission to reproduce CERT Alerts CA=96.05 and CA=96.07, © 1996 by Carnegie Mellon University, is granted by the Software Engineering Institute.

The first CERT Alert was issued after the Jumping the Firewall attack was discovered by the Safe Internet Programming team at Princeton (and fixed by Netscape). The vulnerability was found in February 1996. For our explanation of the DNS-related attack, see Chapter 3.

The second CERT Alert was issued after the Applets Running Wild attack (also referred to in the popular press as the "Princeton class loader attack") was discovered by the Princeton team. The vulnerability was found in March 1996. Our explanation of the Class Loader attack can be found in Chapter 3.

If you would like to be made aware of all future critical security alerts (many of which have nothing at all to do with Java), you can subscribe to the CERT mailing list.

CERT Alert CA-96.05

```
-----BEGIN PGP SIGNED MESSAGE-----
CA-96.05.README
Issue date: March 5, 1996
Revision history
   Mar. 15, 1996    Pointers to Netscape Version 2.01
```

This file is a supplement to CERT advisory CA-96.05, "Java Implementations Can Allow Connections to an Arbitrary Host." We update this file as additional information becomes available.

Note: We recommend checking with your vendor for current MD5 checksum values.After we publish checksums in advisories and READMEs, the checksums may become obsolete because the files they refer to have been updated.

Added March 15, 1996

Although our CA-96.05 CERT advisory does not discuss JavaScript, there have been a series of recent postings to newsgroups concerning a vulnerability in the way Netscape Navigator (Version 2.0) supports JavaScript.

As a clarification to our readers, this problem is different from the problem described in advisory CA-96.05.

Netscape Version 2.01 is now available. This version addresses the Java Applet Security Manager and the JavaScript problems recently discussed. For additional information about these issues and to obtain the new release, please see:

> http://home.netscape.com/eng/mozilla/2.01/relnotes/

-----BEGIN PGP SIGNATURE-----

Version: 2.6.2

iQCVAwUBMaMySnVP+xOt4w7BAQGOqAQAlNgh/CIap5MJaJ9ftsE6mwyVdmi
tiVPoTrS+nmkVJW/zhKM6s2qqcQLUZ5GngQYMGZJHTbs1dzGLrVTIYM6fhO
fCyqjohOnB2R1c2mk6VD1cqxKp2ky96SmaFZffJJqtzO1gu/lAajeVns7Ly
Wk+f4+zM1fdh3dyLYiJ3K3zon4=
=XvEA

-----END PGP SIGNATURE-----

-----BEGIN PGP SIGNED MESSAGE-----

===

CERT(sm) Advisory CA-96.05

March 5, 1996

Topic: Java Implementations Can Allow Connections to an Arbitrary Host

----

The CERT Coordination Center has received reports of a vulnerability in implementations of the Java Applet Security Manager. This vulnerability is present in the Netscape Navigator 2.0 Java implementation and in Release 1.0 of the Java Developer's Kit from Sun Microsystems, Inc. These implementations do not correctly implement the policy that an applet may connect only to the host from which the applet was loaded.

The CERT Coordination Center recommends installing patches from the vendors, and using the workaround described in Section III until patches can be installed.

As we receive additional information relating to this advisory, we will place it in

ftp://info.cert.org/pub/cert_advisories/CA-96.05.README

We encourage you to check our README files regularly for updates on advisories that relate to your site.

I.   Description

     There is a serious security problem with the Netscape
     Navigator 2.0 Java implementation. The vulnerability
     is also present in the Java Developer's Kit 1.0 from
     Sun Microsystems, Inc. The restriction allowing an
     applet to connect only to the host from which it was
     loaded is not properly enforced. This vulnerability,
     combined with the subversion of the DNS system,
     allows an applet to open a connection to an arbitrary
     host on the Internet.

     In these Java implementations, the Applet Security
     Manager allows an applet to connect to any of the IP
     addresses associated with the name of the computer

from which it came. This is a weaker policy than the stated policy and leads to the vulnerability described herein.

II. Impact

Java applets can connect to arbitrary hosts on the Internet, including those presumed to be previously inaccessible, such as hosts behind a firewall. Bugs in any TCP/IP-based network service can then be exploited. In addition, services previously thought to be secure by virtue of their location behind a firewall can be attacked.

III. Solution

To fix this problem, the Applet Security Manager must be more strict in deciding which hosts an applet is allowed to connect to. The Java system needs to take note of the actual IP address that the applet truly came from (getting that numerical address from the applet's packets as the applet is being loaded), and thereafter allow the applet to connect only to that same numerical address.

We urge you to obtain vendor patches as they become available. Until you can install the patches that implement the more strict applet connection restrictions, you should apply the workarounds described in each section below.

A. Netscape users

For Netscape Navigator 2.0, use the following URL to learn more about the problem and how to download and install a patch:

http://home.netscape.com/newsref/std/
java_security.html

Until you install the patch, disable Java using the "Security Preferences" dialog box.

B. Sun users

A patch for Sun's HotJava will be available soon.

Until you can install the patch, disable applet downloading by selecting "Options" then "Security...." In the "Enter desired security mode" menu, select the "No access option.

In addition, select the "Apply security" mode to applet loading" to disable applet loading entirely, regardless of the source of the applet.

C. Both Netscape and Sun users

If you operate an HTTP proxy server, you could also disable applets by refusing to fetch Java ".class" files.

The CERT Coordination Center thanks Drew Dean, Ed Felton, and Dan Wallach of Princeton University for providing information for this advisory. We thank Netscape Communications Corporation, especially Jeff Truehaft, and Sun Microsystems, Inc., especially Marianne Mueller, for their response to this problem.

If you believe that your system has been compromised, contact the CERT Coordination Center or your representative in the Forum of Incident Response and Security Teams (FIRST).

We strongly urge you to encrypt any sensitive information you send by email.The CERT Coordination Center can support a shared DES key and PGP. Contact the CERT staff for more information.

Location of CERT PGP key

        ftp://info.cert.org/pub/CERT_PGP.key

CERT Contact Information

Email   cert@cert.org

Phone   +1 412-268-7090 (24-hour hotline)

            CERT personnel answer 8:30-5:00 p.m. EST

            (GMT-5)/EDT(GMT-4), and are on call for

            emergencies during other hours.

Fax   +1 412-268-6989

Postal address

            CERT Coordination Center

            Software Engineering Institute

            Carnegie Mellon University

            Pittsburgh PA 15213-3890

            USA

To be added to our mailing list for CERT advisories and bulletins, send your email address to

        cert-advisory-request@cert.org

CERT publications, information about FIRST representatives, and other security-related information are available for anonymous FTP from

        ftp://info.cert.org/pub/

CERT advisories and bulletins are also posted on the USENET newsgroup comp.security.announce

Copyright 1996 Carnegie Mellon University

This material may be reproduced and distributed without permission provided it is used for noncommercial purposes and the copyright statement is included.

CERT is a service mark of Carnegie Mellon University.

-----BEGIN PGP SIGNATURE-----

Version: 2.6.2

iQCVAwUBMaMyTXVP+xOt4w7BAQGb/gP/ZKpCOPMt6OUY7tkaATf2y2WGNEnv
4Xf2ElTBhuP8PplrfUrNgeucQfaN4sgXYliwPX9IJpjjEbhG154mGfqOGfo+
RGhXaDSxOKtJaHHgUb7HrNsUIQ3gEy69hiOmdvf6v5FD71XpYDDJRmJcmemq
FF8IwwBBisgd

CvSaJJiERQM=

=1sY8

-----END PGP SIGNATURE-----

CERT Alert CA-96.07

-----BEGIN PGP SIGNED MESSAGE-----

CA-96.07.README

Issue date: March 29, 1996

Revision history

  June 26, 1996   Added additional information
about disabling

                       Java and JavaScript.

  May 16, 1996   Added pointer to Netscape 2.02

  Apr. 1, 1996   Added additional information for
clarification

                   concerning Netscape and Macintosh.

This file is a supplement to CERT advisory CA-96.07, "Weaknesses in Java Bytecode Verifier." We update this file as additional information becomes available.

Note: We recommend checking with your vendor for current MD5 checksum values. After we publish checksums in advisories and READMEs, the checksums may become obsolete because the files they refer to have been updated.

Added June 26, 1996

As a follow up to the May 16th update announcing the avail-ability of Netscape Version 2.02, CERT/CC staff further recommend that sites upgrade to this version and disable Java and JavaScript if these programs are not being used. (This also applies to Netscape Version 3.0b4.)

Added May 16, 1996

Netscape Version 2.02 is now available. We suggest that you upgrade to this version; it addresses the Java Bytecode Verifier problems discussed in the advisory. To get addi-tional information and to obtain the new release, please see

        http://home.netscape.com/eng/mozilla/2.02/relnotes/

Added April 1, 1996

As an addendum to the advisory, we would like to mention that in order to display Netscape's home page, you must have JavaScript enabled.

Along other lines, Macintosh version 2.01 does not support Java, so there is nothing to disable as part of the solu-tion to the problems described in this advisory.

-----BEGIN PGP SIGNATURE-----

Version: 2.6.2

iQCVAwUBMdFOAnVP+xOt4w7BAQFC8gP/e9OjJouLK/nNiGfp6S6unyyJk
YkHqxmIZtX1nJVIARY6t8ZPS+cVeZaLoj6MyzF2OpRirdb+1ArpIABixM
eCh3Xr5EpUQ9+DcMHJjrmLVyp4kMtAVsGZcNuu7/VINE4MtLdVcdn3EBu
9XQxsjci8dgd3UqDdOoF+7/+7wO/mgQI=

=mbwH

-----END PGP SIGNATURE-----

-----BEGIN PGP SIGNED MESSAGE-----

===

CERT(sm) Advisory CA-96.07

March 29, 1996

Topic: Weaknesses in Java Bytecode Verifier

The CERT Coordination Center has received reports of
weaknesses in the bytecode verifier portion of Sun
Microsystems' Java Development Kit (JDK) versions 1.0 and
1.0.1. The JDK is built into Netscape Navigator 2.0 and
2.01. We have not received reports of the exploitation
of this vulnerability.

When applets written with malicious intent are viewed,
those applets can perform any operation that the legitimate user can perform on the machine running the
browser. For example, a maliciously written applet could
remove files from the machine on which the browser is
running—but only if the legitimate user could also.

Problem applets have to be specifically written with malicious intent, and users are at risk only when connecting to
"untrusted" web pages. If you use Java-enabled products on a
closed network or browse the World Wide Web but never connect to "untrusted" web pages, you are not affected.

The CERT staff recommends disabling Java in Netscape
Navigator and not using Sun's appletviewer to browse applets
from untrusted sources until patches are available from
these vendors.

As we receive additional information relating to this advisory, we will place it in

    ftp://info.cert.org/pub/cert_advisories/CA-96.07.README

We encourage you to check our README files regularly for
updates on advisories that relate to your site.

I.   Description

    The Java Programming Language is designed to allow an
    executable computer program, called an applet, to be
    attached to a page viewable by a World Wide Web
    browser. When a user browsing the Web visits that
    page, the applet is automatically downloaded onto the
    user's machine and executed, but only if Java is
    enabled.

    It is possible for an applet to generate and execute
    raw machine code on the machine where the browser is
    running. This means that a maliciously written applet
    can perform any action that the legitimate user can
    perform; for example, an applet can read, delete, or
    change files that the user owns. Because applets are
    loaded and run automatically as a side-effect of vis-
    iting a Web page, someone could "booby-trap" their Web
    page and compromise the machine of anyone visiting

the page. This is the problem described in the Wall
Street Journal on March 26, 1996 ("Researchers Find
Big Security Flaw in Java Language," by Don Clark).

Note: The security enhancements announced by Sun
Microsystems in JDK version 1.0.1 and by
Netscape Communications in Netscape Navigator
version 2.01 do *not* fix this flaw.

II. Impact

If Java is enabled and a Web page containing a maliciously written applet is viewed by any of the vulnerable browsers or Sun's appletviewer, that applet
can perform any operation that the legitimate user
can perform. For example, the applet could read,
delete, or in other ways corrupt the user's files and
any other files the user has access to, such as
/etc/passwd.

III. Solution

We recommend obtaining vendor patches as soon as they
become available. Until you can install the patches,
we urge you to apply the workarounds described below.

A. Java Development Kit users

Sun reports that source-level fixes will be supplied to source licensees in the next few days.
The fixes will also be included in the next JDK
version, v1.0.2, which will be released within the
next several weeks.

The JDK itself is a development kit, and it can
safely be used to develop applets and applications. If you choose to use the appletviewer as a
rudimentary browser, do not use it to browse
applets from untrusted sources until you have
installed the v1.0.2 browser.

B. Netscape users

If you use Netscape 2.0 or 2.01, disable Java using the "Security Preferences" dialog box. You do not need to disable JavaScript as part of this workaround.

For the latest news about fixes for Netscape Navigator, consult the following for details:

http://home.netscape.com/

IV. Information for HotJava (alpha3) users

Sun Microsystems has provided the following information for users of HotJava (alpha3).

Sun made available last year a demonstration version of a browser called "HotJava." That version (alpha3) is proof-of-concept software only, not a product. HotJava (alpha3) uses an entirely different security architecture from JDK 1.0 or JDK 1.0.1. It will not be tested for any reported security vulnerabilities that it might be susceptible to, and Sun neither supports it nor recommends its use as a primary browser. When HotJava is released as a product, it will be based on an up-to-date version of the JDK and fully supported.

The CERT Coordination Center thanks Drew Dean, Ed Felten, and Dan Wallach of Princeton University for providing information for this advisory. We thank Netscape Communications Corporation and Sun Microsystems, Inc. for their response to this problem.

If you believe that your system has been compromised, contact the CERT Coordination Center or your representative in the Forum of Incident Response and Security Teams (FIRST).

We strongly urge you to encrypt any sensitive information you send by email. The CERT Coordination Center can support a shared DES key and PGP. Contact the CERT staff for more information.

Location of CERT PGP key

    ftp://info.cert.org/pub/CERT_PGP.key

CERT Contact Information

Email   cert@cert.org

Phone   +1 412-268-7090 (24-hour hotline)

         CERT personnel answer 8:30-5:00 p.m. EST

         (GMT-5)/EDT(GMT-4), and are on call for

         emergencies during other hours.

Fax   +1 412-268-6989

Postal address

         CERT Coordination Center

         Software Engineering Institute

         Carnegie Mellon University

         Pittsburgh PA 15213-3890

         USA

CERT publications, information about FIRST representatives, and other security-related information are available for anonymous FTP from

         http://www.cert.org/

         ftp://info.cert.org/pub/

CERT advisories and bulletins are also posted on the USENET newsgroup comp.security.announce

To be added to our mailing list for CERT advisories and bulletins, send your email address to

cert-advisory-request@cert.org

Copyright 1996 Carnegie Mellon University

This material may be reproduced and distributed without permission provided it is used for noncommercial purposes and the copyright statement is included.

CERT is a service mark of Carnegie Mellon University.

-----BEGIN PGP SIGNATURE-----

Version: 2.6.2

iQCVAwUBMaMyWXVP+xOt4w7BAQGcsAQAwFe2UxJ5dqHO11CfPzone+3sKmU
YniYLnADXItUV72vOtNJzxJRuHn1ufcGiAAGVif/fFHH3U+BWvDHmzP+INA
RSCOQcZd9qOO3qcxqyrkxeBYt35LuJMuRzAtjAAOsA5PwQWg93u3qri8xEb
w+jPbnrqh5SyZUw

Bw5OUErUD6O=

=cg25

-----END PGP SIGNATURE-----

References

Badger, L. and Kohli, M. (1995). Java: Holds great potential—but also security concerns. *Data Security Letter,* 3:12–15. The *Data Security Letter* (DSL) is published by Trusted Information Systems (TIS).

Bank, J. (1995). Java Security. Web document at URL http://MIT

CERT (1996a). Ca-96.05: Java applet security manager. The CERT Alert can be found in Appendix B.

CERT (1996b). Ca-96.07: Java Security bytecode verifier. The CERT Alert can be found in Appendix B.

Cheswick, W. and Bellovin, S. (1994). *Firewalls and Internet Security.* Addison-Wesley, Reading, MA.

Cornell, G. and Horstmann, C. (1996). *Core Java.* SunSoft Press, Mountain View, CA.

Daconta, M. (1996). *Java for C++ Programmers.* John Wiley & Sons, New York.

Dean, D., Felten, E., and Wallach D. (1996). Java Security: From Hotjava to Netscape and beyond. In *Proceedings of the 1996 IEEE Symposium on Security and Privacy*, Oakland, CA.

DigiCrime. (1996). DigiCrime home page. Website at URL http://www.digicrime.com/ [The authors recommend that you turn Java off before surfing this site.]

Farmer, D. (1996). The SATAN website. Web documents at URL http://www.fish.com/dan/satan.html

Flanagan, D. (1996). *Java in a Nutshell.* O'Reilly & Associates, Sebastopol, CA.

Garfinkle, S. And Spafford, G. (1996). *Practical Unix & Internet Security.* O'Reilly & Associates, Sebastopol, CA. Second edition.

Graffiti (1996). Graffiti. Web document at URL http://whenever .berkley.edu/graffiti

Hughes, L.J. (1995). *Actually Useful Internet Security Techniques*. New Riders, Indianapolis.

LaDue, M. (1996). Hostile Applets home page. Web document at URL http://www.mathtech.edu/~mladu/HostileApplets.html

Lewis, T. (1996). What's wrong with Java? *IEEE Software, 29(6):8*. Lewis's letter to the editor was in response to Java criticism originally printed by him in "The NC phenomena: Scenes from your living room," *IEEE Software, 29(6):8*–10.

OBC (1996). Java Security: Whose business is it? OBC is an acronym for Online Business Consultants. Web document at URL http://www.math.gatech.edu/OBArticle.html

Ritchey, T. (1995). *Java!* New Riders, Indianapolis.

Sams.net (1996). *Java Unleashed*. Sams.net Publishing, Indianapolis.

Schneier, B. (1995). *Applied Cryptography: Protocols, Alogorithms, and Source Code in C*. John Wiley & Sons, New York. Second edition.

Shimomura, T. And Markoff, J. (1996). *Takedown: The Pursuit and Capture of Kevin Mitnick, America's Most Wanted Computer Outlaw— By the Man Who Did It*. Hyperion, New York.

Spafford, E. (1989). The Internet worm program: An analysis. *Computer Communications Review*, 19(1):17–57.

Sun Microsystems (1995). The Java language: a white paper. Web document URL http://java.sun.com. See especially, Chapter 4.

Sun Microsystems (1996a). Frequently asked questions—applet security. Web document at URL http://java.javasoft.com/sfaq/indx.html

Sun Microsystems (1996b). The Java Virtual Machine specification. Web document at URL http://java.sun.com/1.0alpha3/doc/vmspec/vmspec_1.html

Sun Microsystems (1996c). Low-level security in Java. Web document at URL http://java.sun.com/ by Frank Yellin.

Young, Boebert, and Kain (1985). Article in *IEEE Tutorial on Computer Network Security*. IEEE Press.

Index

John Wiley & Sons, Inc. is not responsible for orders placed with MindQ Publishing, Inc.

Six Guidelines for Safer Java Use

Here are six straightforward ways you can make your use of Java more secure. Most are based on common sense. Others require some knowledge of Java. Look for these topics in detail in Chapter 5.

- Know what Web sites you are visiting

- Know your Java environment

- Use up-to-date browsers with the latest security updates

- Keep a lookout for security alerts

- Apply drastic measures if your information is truly critical

- Assess your risks